PROTECTION SPELLS OF A WICKED WITCH

WITCHCRAFT FOR PROTECTION FROM NEGATIVE ENERGY, HARMFUL SPIRITS, AND MAGICAL ATTACKS

THALIA THORNE

HENTOPAN
PUBLISHING

CONTENTS

A Special Offer From Hentopan Publishing

Get this additional book just for joining the Hentopan Launch Squad.

Sometimes you have to make your own justice.
Get your free copy by scanning the QR code with your phone.

INTRODUCTION

The world of magic is not always one of joyfulness and positivity. There are bad people who will try and hurt you, evil spirits that will attach themselves to you, and negative energy that will drain you. In truth, being a witch, or anyone who is attuned to the world of magic and spirits, means you're going to shine like a light in the darkness and attract all those wicked things out there.

If you are going to walk in the world of magic, you must learn to defend yourself.

Some time after I bought my current home fifteen years ago, I was washing my hands, and one of my rings slipped from my finger and fell onto the kitchen counter. It was not the first time soapy water had loosened my ring, but this time I couldn't find it. I finally gave up; it wasn't a family heirloom or anything. But about four months later, I found that ring lying right in the middle of the kitchen counter! Of course, I clean my kitchen counter every day, so I interrogated my family and any friends who had visited, but no one had left it there. I chalked it up to one of those unexplained shoulder shrugs in life, until it started happening with other small items.

There was the time that my glasses, which I always keep on my nightstand, disappeared for two weeks and showed up suddenly on my dresser. I actually wondered briefly if I might've been experiencing early dementia, but my doctor reassured me that I was fine. The problem, I soon realized, was that I had a nasty trickster spirit dwelling in my house! I was on a mission.

Nasty, dark, and even evil spirits lurking in your home bring negative energy into your space, like uninvited guests at a party. They can make you feel sluggish and stuck. I thoroughly cleansed my home; every cabinet, closet, the attic, even under the furniture. I opened all the drawers and put in rosemary sachets. Needless to say, I now maintain a regular practice of warding my home and doing spiritual cleansing.

In this book, I will give you my best spiritual cleansing rituals, banishing spells, and other witchcraftery, so you never have to deal with a pesky spirit rearranging your belongings… or worse!

I must also tell you that I have offended other witches a few times and have had to deal with being cursed. Once, many years ago, I lived alone with my "familiar," a cat named Shade, in a small apartment. At the time, I was a spiritual coach and worked with Runes and Tarot. People of all backgrounds, ages, cults and covens, and even solitaries came to see me for advice. I had some regulars, who were my weekly and bi-weekly clientele.

One day Carrie, a witch I had never met, was my first reading of the day. I welcomed her in and offered her some brew I'd made from my hanging herbs. She walked in slowly, her eyes combing the room. My apartment was peaceful, the walls a calming shade of pale blue. There are always lit candles in my home and at that time I had three indoor rock gardens, complete with trickling water that gave the place a sense of calm and harmony. It seemed like any other day, but as it turned out, it was far from it.

I poured some tea and Carrie asked was what was in it. I proudly told her my recipe for enhancing psychic powers; some peppermint, mugwort, cinnamon, and a bit of orange essence. She picked up a napkin and the teacup and smelled the tea, but then shoved the tea away as if I was trying to poison her. I thought to myself, *This lady is a bit rude*! I asked her why she had come, and she said she was thinking about joining a coven. I told her there were loads of websites that could help her and plenty of social media events publicizing group activities.

Her eyes grew dark, and she shouted at me, "I am sane, but you're in vain!" and she promptly left, slamming my door. I thought, *That witch has some serious issues*, and I chalked it up to another shoulder-shrugging moment, sipped my delicious tea, and went on with my day.

I didn't think much about the strange encounter with Carrie until a few days later. I was going to a friend's house to see his new palomino horse, but my car wouldn't start. It was only a few months old. I had it towed, and the mechanic said it had a short in the ignition. By the end of that week, a whole series of mishaps came my way. The ATM ate my debit card. A neighborhood kid threw a baseball through my kitchen window. Suddenly it hit me! No, not the baseball. I realized Carrie's little "you're in vain" chant had been a nasty and troublesome hex.

Fortunately, I remembered that Carrie had picked up the cloth napkin and the teacup. I took some black string and red yarn—because her hair was red—and quickly made a poppit, binding her hands magically from doing any more harm. I went out in the backyard and torched the napkin, chanting, *"This hex is consumed by fire, begone!"*

Luckily, things went back to normal. As I have thought about it over the years, I realized I could have handled her visit differently. I could have given her specifics about the hundreds of websites that had phone numbers and helpful details about covens for someone looking to join one.

I never saw her again, but I nevertheless apologized by ritual. I lit three magenta candles, burned some sandalwood, and chanted three times: *"Carrie, I apologize for the ill words I have spoken!"* I let the candles burn all the way down so the flame would carry my apology to wherever it needed to go.

Sometimes, I connect to the universe and in return receive a sense of well-being while watching a sunset as it moves to its final destination. Some people call this a spiritual awakening, but when witches open ourselves up to these experiences, we realize it is what being alive is all about. It is about a lifetime of spiritual experiences most humans never realize because their spiritual eyes are closed to their relationship to the universe and to the Elements, which are loving and guiding. To be one with nature, spirit, the universe, the creator, and all that represents a divine presence, is to truly be alive.

Witches and those who are magically inclined are like lights in the darkness. We tend to attract spiritual entities like moths to a flame. Even casting a circle of protection is like sending up a flare. Because we have opened ourselves up spiritually, we are more sensitive and more vulnerable to negative energy and spirits. Cleansing and Protection magic should be a part of every witch's self-care regimen, in the same way we have a regimen to take care of our body.

Throughout history, magical practitioners have used their spiritual powers to enter trances, heal other's minds and bodies, communicate with ancestors, control the weather with rain dances, and yes... combat evil spirits. We understand the spirit world and the earthly world and how to maintain a balance between the two. We use offerings, rituals, spells, and psychic abilities not only for love, health, and money but for protection—and sometimes for revenge.

1

WHY WITCHES NEED PROTECTION MAGIC

P rotection magic is one of the most extensive and oldest forms of magic. Throughout history, every culture known to humankind has had its protective talismans, amulets, and certain charms—referred to as apotropaic charms. Spells and charms to protect against negative energy and bad luck have become a natural practice in most cultures, witches and non-witches alike. Certain taboos, like broken mirrors, black cats, walking under a ladder, and spilled salt, are grounded in protective practices.

In the magical practice of herbs, there are probably as many protective spells as there are spells for good health. This protection manifests in many different ways. Some plants have burrs, thorns, or poisons that act as protective properties. Elements of the Earth, such as grave dirt and soil, are commonly used to avert unwanted energies.

Curses and hexes are sort of like energetic viruses or flu bugs. They affect your own personal energy field with vibrational patterns that create undesirable effects.

There are some differences between a hex and a curse. Curses are not as formal as hexes. Hexes are spells cast with vengeful intent on another person, while curses can be personal, or may also be generational, meaning they've been passed down from your ancestors. Both personal and generational curses can be broken, but just like you don't catch a cold by being around someone with a cold, spells with ill wishes don't automatically turn into curses or hexes. However, if your spiritual immune system is low, you are more susceptible to being cursed or hexed.

A while back, I was conducting a workshop on Tarot, and one of my students asked me if Tarot is considered "black magic." The person was new to witchcraft and still coming to terms with her very religious past. I explained to her that magic is magic, and those who ridicule harmful magic are most likely practicing under the same type of fear, albeit subconsciously.

Protective magic can be practiced in various ways, depending on the need outlined by the circumstances.

They can be preventative spells or precautionary spells, which are more defensive in nature, or there are spells that are more offensive and serious.

Magic, to me, falls into a gray area, because sometimes cursing might be as valuable to a witch as healing and cleansing. People are complicated beings, as are our intentions. In my opinion, spellcasting and all forms of magic are neutral, and only take on what we think of as good or bad properties based on the intent of the practitioner.

Every spell has its intent, reason, place, and time. If someone casts a spell to get a new job, can it also be considered a curse because the witch casting the spell might be putting someone else out of a job? The intentions of a witch when casting a spell depend on the witch's problem, situation, need, and desire.

NEGATIVE ENERGY

The Universe is full of energies, both positive and negative. Usually, people don't intentionally give off negative energy, but it may come down to how complicated their energy sources are within them. I make sure to keep in mind not to become a transmitter or recipient of negative energies. Negative thoughts in the form of being overly critical or quarrelsome, jealous, greedy, and other negative behaviors should be avoided. Evolving into a better person should be a daily activity, and we must realize that our energies affect the environment we live in and vice-versa.

What Are Negative Energies?

Negative energy is the most common problem witches face. Luckily, it's the easiest to deal with, since spiritual cleansing usually eliminates the problem.

Turbulent spirits create negative energies in our world that materialize in many different forms, including but not limited to:

- Recently deceased people or disembodied spirits that have yet to let go of their physical realities.
- A sense of heaviness on your chest or shoulders.
- Headaches, especially around the third eye.
- Ancestors who manifest their spirit forms to bother us, alert us of danger, or help us.
- Otherworldly spirits.
- Thoughts formed by powerful witches, feelers, and thinkers.
- Accumulations of detached emotions, from the inspiring to the dark and dense.
- Trans-auric forms separated from psychopaths

or depressed and damaged people, both living and dead.

- Negative projections from our own minds, intentions, and attitudes.

When Do Negative Energies Strike?

It's important to clear your home of negative energy:

- When you have had a bad day, or you're in a funk. Negative energy amplifies those feelings.
- If you or someone in your family is just getting over a cold or illness. When you're ill, your physical condition coupled with the stress of an illness is weighed down further by negative energy.
- Following a death in the family, divorce, or breakup. Cleansing during grief or heartache can help you process those feelings and move forward.
- After a disagreement or argument with a family member or partner. You both may have said negative things to each other; now that the argument is in the past, it's time to literally clear the air.
- During any major changes or transitions in your life, such as a new job, new relationship, birth of a baby, or new pets—clearing out the

old and providing space for the new energies to come.

- When you feel like you can't make a decision, or you're stuck. If you feel like you're not progressing and want to make some life improvements, evaluate whether the energy in your home is behaving like quicksand.

Signs of Negative Energies

1. Chronic health issues with no solution, either affecting you or a family member.
2. Good opportunities or jobs that are repeatedly snatched away at the final stage of fruition.
3. Desired success seemingly far away and not materializing.
4. Chronic fatigue, lack of focus, and not having the energy to realize opportunities.
5. Decreased creativity.
6. Offending a deity: improper reverence, not following through on a vow.
7. Insults, violence, stress and grief. These weaken us spiritually, leaving us more vulnerable.
8. Uncomfortability in certain places or rooms in your house.
9. Negative or suicidal thoughts.
10. Family members suddenly acting erratic over

the simplest of statements or actions directed at them.

11. Strange and unexplained things happening around the home.

12. Repeated arguments with coworkers or friends.

How to Cleanse and Protect Your Space from Negative Energies

1. Set a new and specific intention for your home. First things first: how do you want your home to make you feel? What do you want to release from your space? For example, "My intention is to release all of my ex's energy and restore this home to peace," or, "My intention is to cleanse my home of all negative energy and bring forth new opportunities for spiritual growth."

2. Cleansing with herbs. For millennia, people from every culture around the globe have been burning herbs to cleanse their spaces from negative energies.

3. Have a fire-safe container. I have a couple of abalone shells, and they are easy to find. Some witches use their cauldrons.

4. Light the end of your herb bundle until it starts to smoke.

5. Fan the smoke in all four corners of your home,

making sure to cover any entrances. I use a peacock feather, but using your hand works just fine, too. I smoke herbs for everything because it makes me feel much better. (Note: If you have any respiratory issues, such as asthma, there are many alternatives. You can use plants and herbal gardens in your home that continually clear negative energy. You just have to create rituals with your intention. There are sage spritzers and soy-based sage candles, too.)

6. Create a crystal grid or place your crystals strategically. Crystals are gifts from Mother Earth. Place two black tourmaline crystals and two hematite crystals around your home.

7. Give your whole house a fresh lemony scent. The smell of fresh lemon is uplifting and invigorating.

8. Let lemon peels simmer in water, and let the steam spread the scent around your home.

9. Slice several lemons and float them in water in small dishes around the house.

10. Use lemon essential oils in your diffuser.

11. Fill your home with the scent of fresh herbs and plants. Lavender, sage, mint, rosemary, and basil fill my home with their lovely aroma while they clear out any negative energy. They are antibacterial and great for cooking, too!

12. Add essential oils to your diffuser, or mix with water in a spray bottle. I also add witch hazel to mine, and the feeling of cleanliness stays all day. It really lifts my spirit.

13. Harness your imaginary powers. Rub your hands together until they become warm, visualize a golden, glowing light in the palms of your hands, and let it expand. Now toss that light around your home, with a set intention of cleansing all energetic congestion.

14. Clear away any clutter. Clutter, dust, and dirt can make your home feel unwelcoming. If there is no clutter, there is no place for negative energies to conglomerate.

15. Weather permitting, open all windows and let the fresh air do its work.

16. Water cleansing is great for light-duty and routine cleansing. You can use spring water, but I like to use moon-blessed water. To make moon-blessed water, leave a container of spring water under a full moon overnight. You can charge your magical tools and sacred spaces and cleanse your home simply by dipping in your fingertips and flicking droplets of the blessed water around.

17. Tip: the best time for a home cleansing is during a waning moon.

SPIRITS

Many witches work with otherworldly entities and spirits. Sometimes you may summon them for good reason, and sometimes they might just drop in unannounced.

Spirits can be found in the most gigantic of trees. Where do you think the superstition "knock on wood" came from? It is said they can also be found on the peaks of mountains or at riversides, deep in the forest or in graves and other solitary places where they usually meet a person who is alone.

Spirits are most active when the massive underground gates swing open at dusk, and an enormous horde of both evil and innocent spirits begin to move freely about the globe. They can influence events in our lives and in society. It has been said that they control draughts, pandemics, floods, and diseases; all bad omens.

When spirits want to cause mayhem with someone who disobeyed their ancestors' orders, they send evil spirits that can humiliate that person and even drive them mad. Some are tortured by the presence of a person who died long ago. Ancestral spirits cannot tolerate a person who is disobedient to the cultural norms of their clan or family.

Sometimes, witches use seances to communicate with the spirit world. A seance is a ceremony that can either be wonderful or a nightmare. How it turns out depends on how well you prepare for it. With well-thought-out planning, your seance can go smoothly. It is smart to expect the unexpected; after all, the deceased are not very predictable. Setting guidelines ahead of time will help ensure that all involved have the best experience possible.

Types of Spirits

As a medium, I sometimes have a challenging time determining whether an apparition is negative or positive, good or evil, vampirish or needy, hurtful or helpful, or some type of complicated hybrid. Psychic vampires are those people who are spiritually harming you, so they unload on you to feel better. Sometimes we feel uncomfortable with energy just because we can feel it, and we are bothered by the space it's occupying.

There are all types of spirits traversing throughout and between all of the realms within the Universe. If we feel their presence, it is usually a blessing rather than a curse. There is no doubt that negative and even evil energies are sauntering around our physical world, but often their effect on us is due to our own insecurities, fears, projections, feelings of victimization, suppressed emotions, or lack of boundaries. It is a loud message to you from the spiritual realm to improve your vibrational energies. We absorb, consume, react to, and attract things we don't understand; we experience unhealthy cravings or other magnetizing unwanted energies.

Spirits can attach themselves to objects, such as clowns, figurines, dolls, and Ouija boards—but that's not all. If you have clothes that have been handed down or bought in a thrift shop, or jewelry, photographs, paintings, and even household objects like furniture, wooden boxes, or musical instruments, these are all popular objects where lost souls can take up residence.

Here are some types of spirits you may encounter:

1. You may encounter non-human spirits that wander like scavengers. Luckily, they're easy to get rid of because they're not looking for a fight. Sometimes, you'll encounter the earthbound dead, a.k.a. ghosts.
2. Servitors or egregores that are no longer being maintained. These are artificial spirits created by magical practitioners. If they aren't properly maintained or dismissed, they will try and maintain their existence by latching on to a person. Many people who have achieved great success have had help from others along the

way, and those in positions of power often have helpers or assistants such as secretaries or interns. Egregores and servitors are similar in their functioning, but they are spiritual energies with quicker ways of manifestation.

3. Demons: Very, very rare. They are usually only a problem if you've been doing ceremonial magic that deals with demons and didn't take enough precautions. However, some choose to use the magic of demons to lead them to power, peace, and extraordinary success. Demons can destroy enemies, provide wisdom and charisma, and satisfy your material desires— those who practice demonic magic claim that material happiness gives rise to spiritual growth.

Signs of Unwanted Spirits Hanging Around

- A picture that won't hang straight or things that keep falling down.
- A feeling of being watched even when you're alone at home.
- Children or pets avoiding specific areas of your home. They're natural ghost detectors.
- Hearing voices of a malevolent nature. Sounds like people whispering.

- Vivid, recurring nightmares.
- Feelings of fatigue—more common from the earthbound dead as they drain a bit of your life energy.
- A feeling kind of like walking through a spider web. You can feel something attached to you, but you can't seem to wipe it off.
- Cold air in one specific room of the house where there is a sudden drop in temperature.
- Putrid odors emerging at a certain time of the day in a specific area.
- A bright light flashing every day at the same time in the same place in your home.
- Your TV all of a sudden turning itself on or off is a sign that a spirit is pulling energy from your power sources.
- You see shadowy figures in your peripheral vision. Spirits tend to move very quickly, so they may look like a shadow flickering or dancing.
- Objects found in weird places where you know you didn't leave them.
- Missing objects are found in strange areas of your home, in places other than where they were left or are usually kept. It's safe to assume that you misplaced an item and forgot, but if it's found somewhere you would never think of

leaving it, then it may be a sign of paranormal hijinks.

- Feeling like someone just tapped you on the shoulder.

How to Rid Your Space of Unwanted Spirits

1. Bang pots and pans, clap your hands, ring bells, or bang a drum—or get creative while walking around your home.
2. Begin at your front door and move clockwise around the inner perimeter of your home.
3. Clap or bang your instrument at the walls until you have completed the circle in your house.
4. Smudge your space with sage.
5. Turn on the lights and open the windows.
6. Ask a deity for help. Meditate and ask the Universe to send a team of angels to help you.
7. Splash blessed water around the corners of your home.
8. Take a bath in Epsom salts or spread sea salt in the corners of your home. Salt repels unwanted spirits but should only be used as a cleanser and not be given to your ancestors.
9. Certain varieties of crystals have protective powers against unwanted spirits. Some act like spiritual shields against negative entities. Place

black tourmaline crystals where you sense the spirit is trying to live or wear a rose quartz crystal as jewelry.

MAGICAL ATTACKS

When magic is used to destroy or harm a person, it is considered a magical attack. These attacks are universal in the "dark arts" and sorcery. They are sometimes hard to counter, but if you are experiencing this, I will tell you what to do here. If it's really bad, however, ask a skilled witch to intercede. Paranoia and fear make these attacks worse. Also, if you try to send the same attack back, and it is repulsed or backfires, it will return to you.

TYPES OF MAGICAL ATTACKS

In a **long-range attack**, someone is made to harm themselves. For instance, a witch may use poppets, send familiars to cause an accident for the victim, or conduct spells to influence dreams. To do this, the witch conducts a ritual in which they work themselves up into a state of rage and then inflict injury upon the poppet, photograph of the person, etc.

In a **short-range attack,** the witch is in close proximity or has physical contact. The witch sends their intent as a powerful energy force, starting from their solar plexus and driving it through their hands, voice, breath, and eyes. The energy force is sent through the victim's body, where it causes problems in their psyche, also known as *psychic vampirism.*

Chaos Magic

Chaos magic is not dark magic, nor should it be confused with magical attacks; it simply uses magic based on whatever practices and ideas are helpful at any given moment, even if it goes against the practices and ideas you have used before.

There are many eclectic witches, who borrow from various sources to create a personal system that their intuition is drawn to. Over time, they create their own routine of rituals that they follow regularly. In chaos magic, a system of routine rituals isn't used. What worked yesterday may mean nothing today. The only thing that matters is what works today. Having a good deal of experience can help you if you are practicing chaos magic because you will know what magical tools work in all types of situations. But chaos magic practitioners are never confined to the concept of coherence or tradition.

In other words, chaos magic is when you practice outside the box, out of the ordinary of every paradigm you normally work with. Once codes are applied, it ceases to be chaos magic. Like all magic, it comes down to the power of belief! If you are not convinced your magic will work, it won't work. It is never as simple as wishing or hoping it will work.

With chaos magic, you can only believe in a tool while you are using it, and then you must cast aside that belief so you will be open to new possibilities. The type of belief necessary for chaotic witchcraft takes experience. For example, traditional witches might use athames, which are ceremonial blades with black handles, for certain rituals, so it makes sense to use them again for a similar ritual. They have standard purposes, but a chaos magician will only use an athame if it suits their current undertaking.

Chaos magic is less complicated in general than traditional ceremonial magic. All of the old occult lessons and specific beliefs about the universe's operations, correspondences, and other principles are considered by chaos magicians to be antiquated voices from ancient Greek wisdom, the Bible, teachings of Kabbalah, etc. None of this matters in chaos magic. Tapping into magic is willful, personal, and psychological; the practitioner simply puts themselves into the right frame of mind, and that is all there is to ritual. Words have no innate power.

Curses

Curses are the usage of magic for selfish and evil purposes and to perform malicious spells to destroy someone financially, mentally, or physically. They can be done using the victim's clothes, a lock of hair, a photograph, or by looking directly into their eyes. Casting hexes or curses has been practiced for hundreds of years.

In all honesty, this is a gray area in witchcraft, in which powerful magic unites with justice and presents a moral quandary for the practitioner. While there are times witches feel compelled to curse someone, it should never be done without careful forethought and consideration.

Curses are usually attacks that send negative energy to our spiritual bodies or chakras. Throughout history, from ancient Egypt to the Bible, people have documented events of curses and hexes in various places around the world.

Types of Curses

There are many different ways for curses to infiltrate a person, family, community, or a nation when the individual or group is most vulnerable. Sometimes, it's when you let your guard down; sometimes, it's from another witch's intent.

Objects and subjects can both be cursed. It was once thought that cursed objects were those that had been looted or stolen from their rightful owners. A cursed object absorbs stories or tragedies, and is thought to bring bad luck.

Quick curses are simple curses that don't take days to perform. Here are some methods to conduct quick curses:

- Spitting on someone would be a direct way of cursing them, but it is also illegal. Instead, you can spit behind or in front of the person, or you can spit on something belonging to the person who you are trying to curse. You can also spit on something you know the person will come into contact with, such as a doorknob or car handle.
- Verbal curses are quick, effective, and easy.
- Write your ill intent on a piece of paper and hide it near the victim. You can doodle a curse sigil on a sticky note or scribe a curse into someone's dirty car window. There need only be a couple of vindictive words to raise a curse.
- Write the victim's name on a piece of paper and burn it.
- Write the person's name on the bottom of your shoe so you step on them everywhere you walk.

- Summon guardian deities or spirits for help.
- Bind, oust, or confuse an enemy who will not leave you be.

Dealing with Curses & Other Magical Attacks

Magical attacks are the hardest to deal with because they are being driven by the attacker's energy and focused on you. Usually, curses will fade on their own, but a determined attacker can keep renewing their curse. This requires cleansing, protection magic, and in my opinion, reversal magic. If you feel you are genuinely a victim of a magical attack, the first thing you should do is protect yourself from further harm.

1. Create a spell using a "magic mirror" to bounce the curse or hex back to its sender.
2. Stay positive and always be kind, polite, and pleasant to others.
3. Avoid being around negative people.
4. Construct a poppet or doll to take your place in being harmed.
5. Cleanse negative energy from your space by burning herbs, oils, and candles. Basil wards off negative magic, and blackthorn works as a spell reversal.
6. Use chakra healing crystals or meditation to lift the spell.

7. Cast a circle of protection, and recharge it on a regular basis. You can recharge your circle with a charged talisman or amulet. This is your psychic protection shield that you draw around you.

8. Your car and property also need protection. Keep a talisman or amulet (Amber protects against psychic attacks) in your car, keep some pink Himalayan salt on your desk at work, and use a magical barrier around your yard.

9. Keep a journal and:

10. Track who you come in contact with and where you go.

11. Track how those persons and places make you feel. If you've been actively attacked, you may feel physical aches and pains when you're around the attacker.

12. Set up early-warning systems.

13. Make magical poppets, dolls, or other decoys to absorb attacks against you.

Evil Eye

The Evil Eye is a legendary curse cast by a witch with the intent of malfeasance. The evil eye is documented as far back as 3,000 BCE in ancient Greek and Roman texts, as well as the Bible and the Quran. It is estimated that 40% of the world's population believes in the evil eye, and many cultures have sought ways to protect against it. Some people use cloves to ward it off.

"My friend," he says, "do not speak loudly, lest some Evil Eye (baskania) put to rout the argument that is to come."

— PLATO

Some cultures consider the evil eye to be accidentally cast by a dead animal. Many believe this explains the tradition of closing the eyes of the dead. When it is cast intentionally, it is often thought to be rooted in envy, as in the envious glare from a hostile person.

Symptoms of Evil Eye

- Physical: The victim experiences chest pain, lethargy, joint aches, and headaches, among other things.
- Mental: The victim's emotions are suddenly out of control, with strange thoughts occurring spontaneously, even including suicidal ideation.
- Spiritual: Intuition and connection to the spirit world is dulled. Magic is weakened.
- You have a run of bad luck.

- You become more accident-prone.
- People start to avoid you—the cursed give off a kind of psychic "smell" that drives other people away.
- People become indifferent or dismissive of you.
- You lose personal items more frequently.
- There is an unconscious change in your personal grooming.
- You experience uncharacteristic compulsions to do things you wouldn't normally do, or to avoid things you normally would do.
- Omens—magical attacks usually have signs you will recognize.
- You have dreams of being pursued or feeling trapped.
- You witness strange animal behavior, especially involving crows (sometimes other birds), rats, insects and lizards.

Protection from Evil Eye

- Be prepared by wearing an evil eye charm that will repel the evil gaze.
- Hang an evil eye bead on your home's entrance.
- Place mirrors near your home's entrance, or carry a hand-held mirror with you to deflect the evil eye.

- Place dill herbs in a bowl by your home's entrance.
- Meditate with clear quartz crystal on your Crown Chakra and speak, "I am safe and protected from the evil eye."
- Cleanse with salt.

Magical Protection Circle

Witches often cast magical circles to perform their spells. Casting a sacred circle cleanses your space of all untoward energies, making it an excellent method for banishing bad juju and protecting you against magical attacks. Conduct daily banishing rituals and make amulets that will prevent most attacks within your sacred circle.

Casting a protective circle against magical attacks can create a barrier against absorbing unwanted energies. Casting a sacred circle can banish and repel any strange presence from your home or space. If you are hearing weird sounds in your house, feeling pockets of cold air, and/or having nightmares, your magic circle will cast out whatever is lingering. Your sacred circle will allow good spirits to come in if you make it so with your intention.

Your sacred circle condenses your magical intent and powers into one area, offering you protection from magical attacks or any other type of harm. It also protects your spells from outside entities and forces. There are both simple and complex methods for casting your magic circle.

The Ritual of the Pentagram Calling in the Four Directions

A pentacle is a pentagram encased in a circle used for protection against magical attacks. The pentagram is documented in history as early as 3000 BCE and found on artifacts in Mesopotamia, Ancient Greece, and Babylonia. So, the pentagram is solidly rooted in ancient history, but what does it mean? In the Jewish Kabbalistic religion, it symbolizes wisdom, justice, understanding, mercy, and transcendent splendor. For the Sumerians, it represented Venus, Saturn, Mars, Mercury, and Jupiter, a.k.a. the "vault of Heaven."

I am telling you about the wonderful and rich history of the pentagram because, for the life of me, I can't understand why people choose to associate it with evil. Most interestingly, famous Greek philosopher and mathematician Pythagoras equated the pentagram with the elements: Earth, Air, Fire, and Water, with Spirit on the top point. His followers were called Pythagoreans, and they viewed the pentagram as perfection in mathematics. Later, the pentagram was known as the "Golden ratio."

The pentagram was labeled as evil when a handful of religious leaders decided to tag it as a sign of heresy. Later, the "Church of Satan," started by Anton LaVey in the 1960s, chose the pentagram as its church's symbol, cementing its association with evil.

Obviously, witches realize how ridiculous it is to take a beautiful symbol of harmony in life and turn it into something people fear. Nowadays, people almost always associate the pentagram with witchcraft, which is fine by me! I love it! It is widely used for protection and other ritual practice. Pythagoras named Spirit as one of the sacred elements and said the pentagram shows all five elements working together in perfect harmony.

Steps for Casting Your Sacred Protection Circle

To call in the four directions, I burn an offering of sage, or you can raise your arms and wave your hands, palms facing outward.

1. Using your broom or besom, sweep outward on your sacred space.
2. Cleanse the entire space.
3. Draw a pentacle with salt and place either crystals or candles on each of the five points.
4. Draw your circle with chalk, salt, or your mind,

and step inside. Note: don't step out until the ritual is finished.

5. Facing East, call upon the element of Water.

6. Moving deosil (meaning sunward or clockwise), call upon each element. "I call upon you, Mother Earth," and continue.

7. Enter a meditative state or trance until you are grounded and centered.

8. Visualize the connection between all five elements, imagining how each one feels on your body and around you: the light of the spirit, the wind's breeze, the sun's warmth, and the earth's cool soil under your feet. (I recommend doing this barefoot).

9. Finish your rotation facing North.

10. You are now ready for spell casting or ritual.

11. Thank each element out loud, and express your gratitude to the elements and to any deities you invited.

12. Moving in a widdershins (counterclockwise) direction, pick up each crystal or candle, one by one, and bid farewell out loud to each of the elements, with utmost sincerity, and close the circle. This is referred to as casting in reverse. "I bid you farewell, most honored water," and so on.

2

IDENTIFYING THE PROBLEM

The first question you need to ask yourself is this: how do you know if you are under a magical attack? There needs to be an assessment of circumstances to rule out other factors before you can label it a magical attack. Is it just a "run of bad luck"? Is a change in lifestyle warranted? Ask yourself the following questions:

- Is there someone in my life I have offended or angered in some way?
- Does that person have the wherewithal to conduct magical spells?
- Is a curse or a hex the only possible reason for the happenings my life?

If you answered "yes" to all three questions, then it's possible you've been hexed or cursed. If that is the case, it is time for protective measures.

HOW TO USE DIVINATION TO IDENTIFY ATTACKS

Divination is the practice of making visible information that is hidden or not immediately obvious. From an observer's point of view, it can seem mystical, magical, or even frightening because you may not understand where these insights are coming from.

Many different traditions and cultures have systems of divination. For instance, Nordic tradition uses runes, and the African sangoma tradition throws bones. All of these systems involve tossing bones or rocks that have been engraved in a specific way. The way they land after being tossed is how the engravings are interpreted.

Like I always say, "Everything comes down to intention!" A working divination system has to be constructed with good intention, so you have positive information with which to work. What good would a divination system be if all of its answers were of gloom and doom? A good system should help you to become the person you want to be.

Tradition has it that some tools, like the runes, are given to people by the goddesses and gods. This is why they are believed to have such deep meaning. Many of my friends think these tried and true systems have more meaning than some of the newer ones. The fact is, if they weren't based on ideas that were true, they would have died out a long time ago.

Many divination practitioners believe divination works because everything is connected through energy and all things have innate intelligence. This means, if you are holding a few crystals on a table, you are connected to the Universe because the Universe is connected to the crystals, in a sense making the crystals living things. If you accept that all things are living, you can be receptive to a higher being's communication with you through all things. All that is left to do is to figure out a method of interpreting the information you are receiving from an object. Once you realize the Earth is an intelligent entity, you can sense the messages that are meant for you. For instance, if you get a flat tire on the way to work, it may be a message that you need to relax and slow down in your life.

There are a variety of methods of divination to choose from in magical practice. Some witches prefer to use multiple types, but you may find your gifts and talents lie in one method more than others. Once you've eliminated all non-magical potential sources of the problem, you can use divination to try to identify spiritual sources.

Many people look to divination as a method for determining if they have been cursed or hexed. If you choose this method, keep in mind that your own anxieties and fears can affect the outcome. It is wiser to have a skilled objective party who doesn't know your worries to conduct the divination. See if this trusted person comes to the same conclusions as you.

A Deck of Cards

Cartomancy, or using a regular playing deck of cards for divination, goes as far back as the early 1300s, but didn't become prominent until the 1800s. Similar to reading tarot cards, each card in a standard deck is assigned a certain meaning. You ask your questions to the cards and then allow your intuition to guide the way. As you pull a card, you tap into your subconscious to discern what the card is trying to tell you.

The simplest way to use a deck of cards for divination is to use it for yes or no questions, ascribing a meaning of yes or no to a color of the card. For example:

- Diamonds or Hearts (red suit cards) mean yes.
- Spades or Clubs (black suit cards) mean no.

Tarot

If you are new to divination, you may think that Tarot card readers are "fortune tellers." However, most Tarot card readers are actually interpreting the likely outcome of a given situation based on the energetic forces currently at work. Think of the Tarot as a vehicle for reflection and self-awareness rather than for telling your fortune. The Tarot is probably one of the most popularly used divination tools in the world today. While they are a bit more complicated than other methods, like tea leaves or pendulums, the Tarot has been a magic method of divination for hundreds of years.

In both Italy and France, the Tarot's original purpose was more for parlor games—not for use as divination tools. Divination with Tarot was popularized in the late 1500s and early 1600s but used far more simplified methods than we use today. By the 1700s, people began assigning particular meanings to each card and offered ideas and suggestions about how Tarot cards could be used for divination purposes.

Today's decks are available in hundreds of designs for you to use your intuition and pick the decks that align with your interests.

Tarot readings are great because they can provide more insight using your intuition than other methods. However, they require a lot of knowledge of the Tarot, and if you're under magical attack, your intuition may be dampened.

The Tarot deck includes 78 cards divided into the Major Arcana and the Minor Arcana. The Major Arcana are 22 trump cards representing ideas, principles, and concepts and are usually more significant than the Minor Arcana. The Minor Arcana are divided into four suits and symbolize the details of the situation depicted by the Tarot spread.

The popular linear three-card Tarot spread is perfect for reading a sequence of events in a linear path: situation, action, and outcome. For this, you will draw three cards:

1. **First card: the source of the problem.** Is it a person in your life? A place where you came in contact with the issue? A spirit?
2. **Second card: the effect of the problem.** Does the card represent a spiritual or a physical symptom? Does it indicate the effect is growing or shrinking? Does it indicate an entity that may be attached to you?

3. **Third card: the solution to the problem.** Do you need to cut ties with someone? Or apologize to them? Do you need to drive someone, or something, away?

Tarot Reading Example with the Question, "Am I Under Magical Attack?"

For instance, let's say you want to know if you are under a magical attack and draw from the tarot deck (left to right), The Five of Swords, the Ten of Swords, and the Six of Pentacles. The Five of Swords can indicate intimidation, bullying, or harassment. Being in the first place of the spread would mean that is the source of your problem. Your middle card, the Ten of Swords, can be interpreted as extreme conflict or disaster. This is definitely starting to look like a magical attack, because the Ten of Swords as the second card means the problem is growing. Now, on the right is the Six of Pentacles. Hooray! This means help is on the way. The Six of Pentacles indicates much-needed assistance bringing relief and generosity.

Pendulums

Since ancient times, witches, healers, and psychics have used pendulums for divination, seeking answers to questions, and locating lost things. They are frequently made from crystal or a gold ring hanging from a gold or silver chain or a silk cord. After asking a yes or no question, the pendulum swings freely and points in the direction of the suggested answer.

Holistic medical doctors hold dowsing pendulums over different parts of their patient's body and observe how it swings. The practitioner is then able to locate where there is an infection. They then hold the pendulum over a range of medications; the remedies most beneficial for the patient pull the pendulum in their direction.

When used for location purposes, the pendulum is hung over a map and slowly moved across it; when it drops or starts to swing, the location is recorded. This has been documented by those looking for oil, gold, people, underground water, and minerals.

Pendulums are easier to use than Tarot but generally only work for simple yes or no questions. A pendulum is a small tool that uses a weighted object such as a crystal or a stone tied to a cord or a string. Mine hangs from a silver chain. Before you use your pendulum, you must calibrate it to your own vibrational energy so that you know before asking any questions which way it will swing to indicate "no," "yes," or "maybe."

While dangling your pendulum, politely ask it to show you a "yes" and closely watch which direction it swings

- circular, vertically, or horizontally. Do the same for "no" and "maybe." Hold the pendulum in your non-dominant hand, meditate and focus on your yes or no questions, and the pendulum will swing in a way that provides you with your answer. Test your pendulum by asking it test questions. For example, "Am I correct to believe my age is (insert your age here)?"

Note: I recommend rather than asking who, what, where, and when questions, start with phrases such as "Am I correct when I say I am under a magical attack?" or "Is it in my best interest to..." or "Am I correct to believe..."

For example, rather than saying, "Should I buy a new car?" say, "Is it in my best interest to buy a new car?" If you need to diagnose a magical attack using a pendulum, ask, "Is there a spirit near me?" "Has someone attacked me magically?" "Was it (insert name here)?"

I also recommend frequently asking your pendulum questions—and not the same ones over and over, or you will need to recalibrate it with easy questions to which you already know the answer.

Cleansing and charging your pendulum continually is very important, as it keeps its energy unburdened and useful. The more you use it, the more often it needs charging and cleansing. Tell your pendulum it is okay to release any energetic baggage it may be carrying. I let my pendulum dangle in sage smoke. I also lay it directly in the soil of my herbal garden. Charge your pendulum in the thick smoke of Palo Santo wood. Place under the moon for charging—for deep cleansing, perform ritual cleansing under a full moon by thanking it for its guidance—and anoint with essential oils.

Reading Tea Leaves

Of the numerous ways to be involved in divination, reading tea leaves is perhaps the most iconic. Tasseography or tasseomancy, also known as reading tea leaves, has only been around since the early 1600s. Historically, women of England's elite class commonly read the fortunes of their servants using tea leaves, even though the technique is thought to have originated in Asia. Tea leaf reading is a method of divination that involves pattern interpretation of leftover tea leaves from a cup of tea. Tea leaf readers identify special shapes and symbols in the tea leaves and then use them to provide insight to answers and to make predictions.

How to Conduct Tea Leaf Reading

While it takes a bit of practice to learn how to read tea leaves accurately, the method itself is quite simple and straightforward. It is best to use a light-colored or white teacup, so you can read the leaves much easier.

Place a pinch of tea (full leaves) into a cup and cover with hot water. Let the leaves steep for five minutes. Then, while enjoying your cup of tea, meditate on what you want to learn from your reading as you sip the tea.

When there is just a small amount of liquid left, and the tea leaves sit on the bottom of the cup, the person drinking the tea should quickly swish the liquid clockwise in a circle three times. This will leave some of the tea leaves pressed against the sides of the teacup, with the remaining leaves on the bottom.

Turn the teacup upside down and let the liquid drain. Next, flip the cup back over, and read the tea leaves. You're looking for tea leaves that have formed into recognizable shapes or clusters. These could come in the form of animals, objects, letters, numbers, or even mythical beings. What each tea cluster means will be up to you based on the question you asked. The closer the leaves appear to the rim, the sooner the events depicted by the reading will occur. The closer to the bottom, the further into the future the events will occur.

It is also key to pay attention to the size of the shapes and symbols that form and how close or far away they are from one another. Using your intuition, try to get the full picture of the patterns, as well as the individual tea leaf symbols.

Scrying

Scrying, also known as crystal gazing, means predicting future or distant events based on visions seen in a crystal ball, polished metal, and reflections in water, and was practiced by ancient humans who interpreted these visions as an appearance from the spirit world. Scrying became popular as far back as the 5th century AD and was quickly condemned by the Church in medieval times as the work of the devil.

Crystal Balls

Crystal balls have been used for millennia for scrying. The first people to use crystal balls would meditate and allow their subconscious mind to connect to the spiritual realm and see hints of the past, present, and/or future. Some believe you have to be an experienced psychic to read crystal balls, but true crystal balls can see in all directions once the Seer obtains the ability. This practice of gazing into a translucent or reflective surface to obtain prophetic insight, now known as scrying, can be used on anything, including mirrors, water, blood, and even oil, but crystal balls are still the most common tool for this type of divination.

By focusing on the crystal, which is usually made of glass (sometimes clouded), you can interpret the visions that foretell aspects of the past, present, and future. The crystal ball uses your psyche to exercise your intuition. As you practice, and your ability to see other ephemeral visions is enhanced, you will begin to see parts of shapes and symbols in the crystal ball, and these will slowly become more and more like real visions.

Fire Scrying

Fire scrying is done by gazing into a fire's flames to see what type of visions appear. As with all forms of scrying, it is all about paying attention to your intuition. Focus on the flames, relax your mind, and receive the messages about what you need answered.

Watch the fire dancing and flickering, and look into the flames for images. Some people see specific and clear images, while others see hints of shapes in the shadows. Look for repeating patterns and images that trigger a sense of familiarity. You may also be able to interpret sounds you hear, which are more than just the wood crackling, embers snapping, or flames roaring. Some even hear faint voices speaking or singing in the fire.

Water Scrying

Water scrying, or hydromancy, is very popular and can be done in any body of water, from a lake to a bowl. Nostradamus used a large bowl of water for scrying and induced himself into a trance so he could interpret his visions. Some of my witch friends like to read the reflections of the moon during water scrying. This is a great method for lunar lovers.

Hydromancy is accomplished by placing a bowl of water in front of you and then using your wand to create a ripple in the water. Traditionally, wands are made from laurel, hazel, or bay tree branches, as they have sap or resin dried on their ends. You can use that sap to rub around the lip of the bowl, which will create a resonating sound that you can incorporate into your scrying.

Mirror Scrying

Mirrors are easy to take with you, so they are a very practical tool for scrying. If you choose to practice mirror scrying, look for a mirror with a black backing because it reflects better. For mirror scrying, light a candle and completely relax your mind, ridding it of any mundane thoughts. Visualize those tedious thoughts as solid objects, whirling around your head and then stopping and dropping to the floor. Put yourself into a trance and stare into the mirror. Focus on the reflection in the mirror and the flickering candlelight and its occasional whirls of smoke. Let your eyes remain relaxed, don't strain your vision trying to see something, let the images come to you.

Afterward, record any images or feelings you had during the session. Messages can come from other realms, and sometimes we don't recognize them for what they are. You might even receive a message meant for someone close to you, so if it doesn't apply to you, meditate on who could be the intended recipient.

3

SPIRITUAL CLEANSING

For me, spiritual cleansing was a life-changing activity! Spiritual cleansing removes negative energy from your environment and yourself. In the same way we have to brush our teeth and take a shower to remove any dirt that has accumulated on our bodies, it is just as important to keep our spirit clean. Negative energy is all around us, and it attaches itself to us as we go about our daily activities. We encounter it when we go to work, grocery store, shopping mall, etc.

Most of us have heard the saying "Cleanliness is next to godliness." Spiritual advancement is also about cleansing yourself of any unclean or negative energies hiding within you. It is about unblocking and aligning your beliefs and patterns of thought. Beliefs can block you and stifle your powers. After a spiritual cleansing, you are better able to connect to your authentic self and your passions. It is the ultimate freedom from the constraints of society and earthly confinement.

Even though we don't have the technology to measure negative energy, you most likely know what it feels like. It can come from being around negative people or even from your own psyche. It can settle in as fatigue or exhaustion, both physically and mentally. Negative energy is self-perpetuating, therefore, it breeds and attracts more negativity. Learning how to get rid of it is essential to your health and your happiness.

Before learning how to do spiritual cleansing, you need to know the sources of negativity that might be affecting you. Spiritual cleansing gets rid of negative energy and can remove spirits attached to you. Since witches and magic users tend to be affected by negative energy more than other people, it should be done regularly, at least once per week.

These three sources may be causing your feelings of negativity:

1. **Negative People**: We can very much sense when we are around a positive or negative person's energy. We sense sadness, anger, lethargy, and other projected negative energies. We are experienced at reading nonverbal and

verbal cues even when the person isn't openly expressing them.

2. **Negative Environments**: Sometimes, we feel very uncomfortable in an environment, much like we feel very comfortable in others. We feel much better visiting a close friend than sitting in the waiting room at the dentist's office. Those anxious and uncomfortable notions attach themselves to your psyche, but your physical environment also plays a big part in negative energy accumulation. This clutter can actually interfere with your sleep, impact your mood, and create stress. When you are uncomfortable in an environment, that means it probably has negative energy.

3. **Negative Self-Talk**: Self-talk is your internal monologue, or the way you narrate your life—it is the thoughts that run through your head. Negative self-talk can be harmful to your physical, mental, and spiritual well-being. Studies have shown that positive thinkers are less susceptible to cardiovascular problems, the common cold, and depression, and actually live longer!

GROUNDING

Most people who have practiced any type of spiritualism or magic have heard references to the practices of centering and grounding. Grounding or Earthing power is a way to connect yourself personally with the Earth's energy. When feeling stressed or anxious, grounding techniques are an excellent way to release any energy overload from within yourself. If you are lacking energy, grounding is an excellent way to pull the Earth's energy and provide you with enough while protecting your own supply.

If you fail to center yourself before practicing magic, you might feel jittery, odd, or a bit off-kilter. What happens is that you have amped up your vibrational energy, increased with ritual, and now you're on overload. This is when grounding is necessary. It is a way to rid yourself of excess energy, as well as gain energy when feeling depleted. Once you learn how to ground yourself, you will know how to find balance when you need it.

Instead of cloaking yourself with the energy, as you do when centering yourself (see below), you are going to push energy out of you with your hands.

To start, comfortably sit or lie still with your hands flat on the ground. Take three deep breaths in through your nose and out through pursed lips while picturing energy, as if it were visible electricity, flowing through you and out into the ground. Do the opposite if you are in need of an energy boost. You can also visualize yourself as a tree, with your roots deep in the ground, and visualize the energy flowing through your trunk. Keep meditating on the energy flow until you feel grounded.

Another method for grounding if you feel an energy overload (which can also cause insomnia) is to keep a crystal or stone in your pocket and let it absorb the energy. Or, you can keep a pot of dirt outside of your front door, and when you feel an energy overload, dig your hands deep in the soil and transfer the energy (I call mine "angry dirt" because of all the energy it has absorbed). You can also create a mantra, "Aaaand it's out of here!" and simply shout it to release energy whenever you need to.

CENTERING

Centering is essential for magical practices involving energy work. Many magical traditions have their own methods for centering. I will share mine here with you. To start, first complete the grounding exercise. Next, find a space where you will not be disturbed. Turn off your phone and all other electronic devices, and lock the door. Sit comfortably or lie down, but don't get so relaxed that you fall asleep! Once you are comfortably positioned, take three deep breaths and exhale, so you are breathing evenly. You can count to four, inhaling and exhaling, or chant a tone as simple as "Om" while deep breathing. The more you practice breathing exercises, the easier they will become.

Once your breathing is even and regulated, start visualizing the energy by rubbing your hands together, creating friction, and then move them an inch apart. You should be able to feel the energy charge as a tingling sensation. Again, with practice, you will get to know this energy. Once you have mastered this technique, you will then be able to manipulate the energy. Close your eyes and pay attention to how it feels. Visualize it contracting and expanding like a balloon or stretching it out like taffy between your hands. Work with the energy until you can cloak your body with it. With a good deal of experience and practice, you will be able to center yourself wherever you are.

Visualize your energy centering in your body. Your center is your place of balance and your center of gravity. Your center lies directly between your breastbone and your navel. You might also be aware of a place in your body where you store personal energy. To locate this place, visualize something you love passionately; when you feel this passion swelling, pinpoint its location in your body. This is your center. Now, sitting or lying in the same way you did for your grounding technique, relax your emotional, physical, and mental awareness at your body's center. Sit still for a few moments and realize you are both grounded and centered.

SHIELDING

Use this simple shielding method to protect yourself from magical attacks, and from depleting, dangerous, or counter-productive energies. Consider the centering and grounding exercises you just read about. Visualize a clear bubble or sphere of light surrounding your whole body. Imagine its movement as you move and that it is protecting you. Visualize an actual shield protecting you. With enough practice, you can learn how to shield your car, home, altar, and even your bed.

When forming your energy shield, imagine the exterior of it as being mirrored, so it will repel any bad energies or negative aspects back to its original sender. Think of it like a window tint that lets a bit of light in, but not enough to harm you. If you are subject to psychic vampires or other big-time energy suckers, then you will need to know how to use shielding techniques.

SPIRITUAL CLEANSING SPELLS

Spiritual Protection Bath Spell

Spiritual cleansing rituals have been around since ancient times. Cleansing and bathing rituals have been a documented tradition in ancient Greece and ancient Rome, as well as India, Asia, and the Middle East. Water is known as the universal solvent because of its ability to dissolve more things than any other liquid. Wherever water flows, over our bodies and skin, inside of plants and trees, through the ground, it carries energy and substances along with it. Herbs, minerals, and essential oils can all be added to water to improve spiritual health and wellness.

I really enjoy soaking up the healing energy of a warm bath—but spiritual bathing and magical bathing are not the same thing. A magical bath with salt and herbs brings about the protective energy you need. There are many water herbal combinations in a magical protection bath. I recommend hyssop, basil, hawthorn, cinnamon, rosemary, and nutmeg. Just do your homework to make sure the herbs you pick are safe for bathing, and decide which blends work best for you.

Salt water is used by many witches for many reasons. One of the most common reasons is for protection. As a witch who loves working with water, I use a lot of sea salt. You can always use a little sea salt in your magic. It is great in a magical protection bath to protect your sacred space and also for warding rituals. All you have to do is add four pinches of sea salt to water, call upon the element of Water for protection, and stir in a clockwise direction. You can then charge your tools, draw protective pentagrams or runes, and drip some over your doorsteps to keep out unwanted energies.

Protection bathing rituals revitalize your aura, cleanse and unblock your chakras, and leave you in a positive and present state of mind. Your spirit is regenerated, not just from soaking in warm soapy water, but from the vibrational energies imparted by the powerful herbs, oils, or crystals you have added to your bathwater.

Just as you take a regular bath to clean your body, using shampoo, soap, and water, a spiritual bath works to cleanse the spirit and your mind. Using magically powerful ingredients that charge the bathwater with healing energies, protection baths work by removing blockages, pain, and hurtful situations, such as those accumulated from magical attacks.

WHEN TO PERFORM THE SPELL

Twice per month

HOW LONG IT TAKES

3 hours herbal preparation
1 hour for the bathing ritual

WHAT YOU'LL NEED

- Basil: Protective
- Cinnamon: Stops quarrels and dissension
- Hyssop: Cleansing
- Nutmeg: Removes negative thoughts
- Black candles: Psychic protection
- Sandalwood incense: Protective
- Epsom salt: Unblocks chakras
- Optional: Rose petals, bay leaves

STEPS

1. Add the herbs for your ritual bath to 3 liters of boiling water.
2. Let the herbs steep in the boiling water for 15 minutes, and then let it simmer for two hours. Let cool.

3. First, scrub your bathtub thoroughly to make sure it is completely clean.

4. Set your intention that this is your time, and you will not let yourself be disturbed by phone calls, text messages, or visitors for 45 minutes to an hour.

5. Rinse yourself off in the shower first, without the use of any soaps, body washes, or other cleansing agents, as they should not be used in spiritual bathing.

6. Fill your bathtub with warm water that is a comfortable temperature for you.

7. While your tub is filling with water, gather your ingredients according to your intention.

8. Bring the pot with the blended herbs to your tub and prepare to begin the ritual.

9. Light a few candles, pour yourself a glass of wine or tea, and play some ambient music (let your intuition guide you when deciding your environment).

10. Step into the bath, pour the herbal ritual water from the neck down and soak for around 30 minutes.

11. As you relax in the water, release all unwelcome thoughts, and focus your intention on letting go of all negativity. Visualize the stress leaving

your body as the negativity rises with the
vapors of the herbs.

12. Focus on the scents, slowly breathing in their
    aroma.

13. Thank the water and the herbs for participating
    in the ritual.

14. If you have time, air dry your body, letting the
    ritual waters dry into your skin. **Note:** Wait a
    full 24 hours before showering again, as the
    protection herbs linger in your auric field.

Spiritual Egg Cleansing Spell

Eggs are frequently used in protection magic. There are
many ways that eggs are used in cleansing rituals. In
Hoodoo, a black hen egg is normally used. In American
folk magic, witches use ground-down eggshells called
Cascarilla powder. You can make some by washing out
some eggshells, letting them dry, and then grinding
them into a powder using a mortar and pestle. Sprinkle
the Cascarilla powder around your crystals, candles,
and put some in your witch's bottles and other items
you want to cleanse and protect. While I don't recommend throwing a dozen eggs at your home, do throw
one on the roof to protect it.

Also referred to as "limpia" or "oomancy," spiritual egg
cleansing is an ancient healing ritual originating in

Ancient Rome, Greece, Mesoamerica, and Mexico. Oomancy was performed by Native Americas, Polynesian, African, the ancient druids, and Arabic cultures.

It can ease suffering by ridding the mind and body of emotional and spiritual blocks that affect the soul. It is a cleansing practice used to clean the body, mind, and soul of negative energy. It also removes the effects from magical attacks, evil eye, magic spells, fears, bad luck, addiction, chakra imbalances, bad karma, and confusion. It is such a powerful practice that it can help with illness and remove sickness of the spirit. However, this doesn't mean that you shouldn't still see your doctor for wellness checks.

WHEN TO PERFORM THE SPELL

Twice per month

HOW LONG IT TAKES

All day

WHAT YOU'LL NEED

- White candle
- 1 egg
- Glass of water

- Sage

CHANT

"I have chosen to cleanse myself and release all energies, thoughts, and beings that no longer serve my best
interest. Please make of this egg a vessel to vacuum
across all of the realms of my existence, across all of the
universes and all of my lifetimes. I ask that any energy
less than love be released for the greater good of all. It
is done."

STEPS

1. Take a spiritual bath as described above.
2. Place your egg on your altar along with the
   glass of water until both are at room
   temperature.
3. Practice your grounding and centering
   exercises.
4. Wave your egg over the candle (not closely)
   three times.
5. Pass your egg through the smoke of burning
   sage.
6. Chant the above chant while holding the egg
   overhead.
7. Starting with your head, roll the egg over your

body, ending with your feet, making sure to cover your entire body.

8. Crack your egg into your glass of water.

9. Read your egg in the same fashion as described for tea leaf reading.

10. If the egg settles in the center of the water in the glass, you have protection against the "evil eye."

11. Bubbles on the bottom or around the rim mean your ancestors are watching and absorbing any evil, magical attack, or negativity thrown at you.

12. If your egg yolk breaks, it could mean you have been hexed and need to repeat the process until the yolk does not break.

13. With your intuition, look for signs and symbols that hold meaning.

Spiritual Cleansing for the Home Spell

In the past, spiritual home cleaning was conducted when the person or family first moved in. But with what we know about negative energy these days, I suggest making it part of your monthly deep clean. Leave your old besom (broom) at your former home, if you are moving into a new home, so that none of your troubles will follow.

When we set up our homes, we generally want them to be a reflection of what makes us feel peaceful, joyful, and safe. It helps us to connect with our authenticity. Being connected to our authentic selves is essential for magic and for manifesting our desires. A magically protected home allows you to live in a comfortable place for you and your spirit.

One of the biggest ways negative energy gets stuck in your home is the staleness that has accumulated through your belongings. The best way to banish these heavy feelings is to clean out the clutter. It doesn't have to be a massive undertaking. Pace yourself, do one room at a time, recycle, donate, and throw away! Every time I reduce the clutter in my space, I can literally feel the weight being lifted off of me. Sometimes just finding boxes or baskets to hold items that I have out gives me a sense of order and calmness. I try to give my items their own home within my home.

If you are moving into a new home, treat it like you do a magical body cleanse. It is an ideal chance to flush out the negative and make room for the new. Give your new home a good once-over before you even start to move in. Wash the floors and windows, and sweep out any sawdust or cobwebs as you visualize sweeping away the past and allowing glowing possibilities of your future to shine through. Whoever lived there before has left vibrations related to their tribulations, memories, and struggles. Sweep away all, to be forgotten for your new fresh start. Visualize what your life will be like within the walls of your new home; happy, joyous, and free.

If you are sensing a magical attack or a haunting, you can perform a cleansing ritual to ask the specter to leave. If it's a negative energy build-up, you can cleanse. Floor washes affect those who walk on the clean floors. If there is someone in particular you want to influence, you can cleanse where you know they will walk. Before casting this spell, be sure your home is tidy.

WHEN TO PERFORM THE SPELL

Once per month or as needed

HOW LONG IT TAKES

1- 2 hours

WHAT YOU'LL NEED

- 20 drops lemongrass oil
- 15 drops lemon oil
- 15 drops rose oil
- 15 drops vetiver oil

- Raw apple cider vinegar
- Spring water
- Mop and bucket
- Sage
- Salt

CHANT

"In this home where loved ones live,
Cleanse and protect it all.
Bless every window and every door,
All of the ceiling and all of the floor.
It is done."

STEPS

1. Mix oils and ½ water, ½ raw apple cider vinegar in a clean mop bucket (preferably a new one, for the first time, and then only use that bucket for spiritual cleansing).
2. Wash down the walls and floors. If there is wall-to-wall carpeting, spritz a freshly vacuumed rug with the solution.
3. While washing, mopping, and spritzing, chant or make a song out of the above chant.
4. Wash from the top floor to the bottom floor and from the back to the front.

5. If you have a front yard, take some of the formula and throw it to the east in front of your house.
6. If you feel you are under a magical attack, bury four unopened boxes of lye in the four corners of your yard.
7. Come right back in without speaking to anyone.
8. Place a pinch of salt in every corner of your home.
9. Cleanse the entire house with sage.

INCENSE FOR SPIRITUAL CLEANSING

Incense is an aromatic biological material that smokes when burnt. It is usually made from essential oils, herbs, or other plant matter to give it a specific scent. From preparing altars to cleansing your sacred space, incense has been used in ritual for hundreds of years, all the way back to the Ancient Egyptians fumigating tombs to rid them of the smell of death. Traces of myrrh and frankincense have been documented in the Ancient Egyptian burial chambers. It has also been traced back to Asia and India as early as the 4th century AD, where it was used for purification, protection against evil, religious ceremonies, and prayer. Most interestingly, in the 12th century, buildings in China were believed to be designed specifically for the burning of incense. All in all, incense has a rich history in almost every culture around the globe.

Incense Benefits

1. **Cleanses and rids negative energy:** You can literally feel a change in the energy of a space. Tension flees and takes conflict along with it. I intuitively know what type of incense I am going to burn, and as soon as I wave it in the air, I can almost see the bad juju making a run for it. Use your incense in a sweeping motion to sweep out anything you don't need clinging to your stuff.

2. **Spirituality practices:** Incense has a long and rich history that remains hugely popular today. Incense can cleanse your chakras, cleanse your home of negative energy, and protect you from magical attacks. Use it when working with Tarot, crystals, and divination spell work.

3. **Helps you to focus by calming the body:** Use for preparation for meditation, journaling, dream recall, and any other ritual where you need to connect to your higher self with a calming attitude.

4. **Anxiety reduction:** Incense works to alleviate anxiety, regulates your nervous system, and

self-soothes. It stimulates a release of serotonin (the feel-good chemical of the brain). Sandalwood will slow your heart rate, and lavender will help you sleep.

5. **Aphrodisiac qualities:** Certain scents stimulate your sexual desires and needs for touch and other forms of human connection. Vanilla, rose, and jasmine are the go-tos for getting in the mood.

6. **Yoga or stretching exercises:** Set your intention and create a sacred space for your meditation practices. You can create a healing environment with sage, frankincense, and sandalwood.

7. **Boosts your creativity:** Kickstarts your creative juices. Dragon's blood or any other incense that corresponds with earth and fire will help you to set your intention.

8. **Health benefits:** Your body naturally reacts to certain aromas in a positive way. It can reduce fatigue, work as a mood stabilizer, alleviate headaches, and soothe your mind.

Types of Incense

If your intuition is calling for incense, there are different types to choose from. Cones, sticks, and powders are all methods for welcoming some sweet-scented magic into your practice.

- **Incense sticks/joss sticks:** Bamboo sticks coated with essential oils or incense.
- **Resins:** Nature-made and tapped right from the tree. This type of incense is commonly used in ceremonies and churches.
- **Incense cones:** Made from flammable materials combined with aromatic essential oils that are pinched together and dried in a cone shape.
- **Incense coils:** This is a spiral shaped coil, similar to the incense stick, only it lasts much longer.
- **Incense powders:** Plant matter, ground down woods, essential oils and resins combined into powder form.

Incense is made of plants, woods, and other kinds of biomaterials made of natural matter. Ancient forms were made of resins, oils, and woods. They have since evolved into additional fragrances, herbs, and adhesive powder.

Each incense type has a particular lighting method, and familiarizing yourself with how each type burns adds richness to your rituals. Some types are easier than others; for instance, sticks and cones are easier to burn than powders and resins. The good news is that there are endless amounts of incense paraphernalia out there to choose from.

Remember: SAFETY FIRST! Don't leave your incense unattended, and never leave it next to anything combustible.

- **How to use incense sticks:** A.k.a. joss sticks, these are the most commonly used type of incense for burning. You simply place it on an incense holder and light the end of it. As soon as it flames, blow it out and let the smoke do the rest.
- **How to use incense cones:** Cones are major cleansers, belting out wonderful aromas. Always have the point facing heavenwards. Light the point, blow out the flame. These don't last quite as long as the other types but are big cleansers.
- **How to burn incense powder:** There are specialized discs of charcoal just for incense burning. Hold your flame over the charcoal until it lights. Wait until the coal is burning. Sprinkle the powder over some charcoal to burn it. **A FIREPROOF CONTAINER IS A MUST.** The powders burn quickly, so for ritual purposes, keep sprinkling.

- **How to use coil incense**: Perfect for ritual and ceremony in larger spaces. They work like those mosquito repellent coils. There are special holders for coil incense, as you need large and flat non-flammable holders.
- **How to put out incense**: Incense usually burns itself out. If you want to snuff it for magical purposes, or because you don't have the time to wait for it to burn out, use water—but then you usually can't relight it. Cut the end off or use a proper snuffer.
- **Incense burners**: These are usually made of clay or ceramic. They come in a huge range of styles, from the super simple to the super ornate. Use your intuition and pick the ones you are drawn to.

Magical Properties of Incense

There are many types of incense, and their magical properties differ. Here are some of my favorites:

- **Amber**: Calling the truth and comfort. Amber is all fire and air and helps you to dive deep into your inner wisdom.
- **Bergamot**: Courage, motivation, assertion, power, and sweetness.

- **Cedar**: Purification and cleansing a home or sacred space.
- **Cinnamon**: Protection, grounding, and invoking our inner power.
- **Citrus**: Energizing, confidence, sunshine.
- **Clove**: Focus, memory improvement, pain relief.
- **Coconut**: Chastity and calmness.
- **Dragon's Blood**: Courage, power, appetite, and balance.
- **Eucalyptus**: Cleanses home and space, enlightenment, and respiratory wellness.
- **Frankincense**: Money, power, purification.
- **Ginger**: Digestion, spell casting, brings heat and energy-boosting.
- **Green tea**: Cleanses the home of viruses and bacteria and promotes a healthy nervous system.
- **Jasmine**: Increases self-esteem, love, creativity.
- **Lavender**: Nurturance, rest, softness, sleep.
- **Lemongrass**: Mood lifter, focus, provides energy when fatigued.
- **Myrrh**: Ancient scent used for purification, friendships, and protection.
- **Palo santo**: Ancient healing properties, energetic protection, rids space of negative energy.

- **Pine**: Protection, warms the soul, cleansing, winter, earthy.
- **Rose**: Love, fertility, connection.
- **Patchouli**: Drawing money, attraction spells, and material pleasures.
- **Sandalwood**: Removes all types of negative energy; used for healing and promoting peace.
- **Vanilla**: Soothing, mood lifter, dissolves anger, cools your space.
- **White Sage**: Purification, rids bad energy, heals mind, body, and soul.
- **Ylang Ylang**: Connected to high degrees of euphoria.

4

PROTECTION MAGIC

In our everyday life, and especially while training as a magical practitioner, we can fall victim to outside powers. We have already discussed the importance of grounding, centering, and shielding, but sometimes that's not enough. Sometimes, we have to invoke or create some type of magical protection. The best time to learn protection magic is long before you need it. We live in a Universe where all things contain a spirit, and we don't necessarily get along with all of them every day.

PROTECTING YOURSELF

The simple shielding method from Chapter Two is a temporary measure; it is like putting up your spiritual dukes. It definitely lets those around you know you feel threatened. Acting or feeling defensive can magnify an issue that could have been otherwise avoided. If you are early in your training as a witch, most problems can be remedied with grounding, centering, and shielding or banishing. I must caution you, if you are feeling empty or drained, and even small things seem threatening, it could be the result of your own lack of inner power and might not come from outside.

Magic can't stop physical attacks, but it can guide your intuition, so you steer clear of bad situations. Spiritual attacks are seldom intentional. However, we live in a spiritual world, where there are continuous interactions between our own spirits and those of others. Often an angry, upset, or annoyed person lashes out unintentionally. If you are a very sensitive person, this is no fun. This is a common occurrence, as in the case of road rage.

The more time spent developing your spiritual core, the less time you will have to spend defending yourself. Avoiding troublesome situations is always better than fighting them. But there will be times when running away is not the answer, and you must protect yourself.

Protective Charm Bag Spell

Creating a protective charm bag is a great way to practice magic and cherish your magical tools. Keep it with you always as a way to repel negativity and attract the kind of energy you want in your life. Charm bags are more than just carrying a talisman or an amulet. A charm bag is a tangible place to store invisible spirits and energies to assist you in your practice. The magic only stays active while the bag stays intact. If you open it, the energy escapes, and the bag loses its effectiveness for any needs in the future.

The charm bag is made of fabric and stuffed with sacred objects and herbs. Sewing, weaving, and embroidery have been closely connected to witchcraft since ancient times. Weavers were also known as enchantresses, and the goddess Isis was a protector of yarn.

Consecrations, rituals, and ceremonies are used to amplify power of the bag. It is important to choose the right color and to use natural fabrics, such as silk, hemp, or flannel. I recommend using black fabric for this spell bag for its corresponding protective measures. The color black corresponds with protection, uncrossing, and warding off any negative vibes trying to enter into your space.

This spell should be cast during a dark moon, which occurs right before a new moon. The dark moon is waning, and is barely illuminated. The dark moon represents introspection, stillness, soul searching, meditation, and baneful magic. It's a time for traveling inside ourselves, divination, and reflection. The dark moon is one of my favorite times to work magic. It is a time when the moon shrinks and shrinks until it disappears from the sky.

Different witchcraft traditions work their magic at different times during the dark moon. I feel it's most powerful when you can't see it at all. Some of my witch-mates like to work on the last two days before the arrival of the new moon. I suggest using your intuition and taking note of your feelings during each of the dark moon days to determine when you feel it's most powerful.

WHEN TO PERFORM THE SPELL

Daytime or nighttime. Most powerful when made during a dark moon.

WHAT YOU'LL NEED

- 1 black candle: Protection
- Coarse sea salt: Protection

- Black natural fabric: Protection
- Needle and black thread
- Incense of juniper and rosemary
- Water

HOW LONG IT TAKES

30 minutes

CHANT

"This charm bag is made sacred with the powers
of Air.
This charm bag is made sacred with the powers
of Fire.
This charm bag is made sacred with the powers
of the Earth.
This charm bag is made sacred with the powers
of Water.
This sacred charm bag will serve (your name) so
that I will be protected.
It is done."

STEPS

1. Cut a square of black fabric. You must do this

yourself because you are the one being armed with magic.

2. Rinse your fabric in saltwater and let dry.
3. Hand sew three corners, leaving an opening in the top.
4. Gather the rest of your materials.
5. Ground and center yourself.
6. Cast a magic circle with an operational altar inside.
7. Light your black candle while calling forth protection from negative and dark forces.
8. Light your incense and fan the smoke over the salt.
9. Mix the salt and aromatics with your hands while reciting your protective chant.
10. When you feel the salt is efficiently charged, pour it into the bag.
11. Sew the bag closed.

Rue Water Spell

Rue is one of the most popular herbs used in protection magic. Whether it's banishing magic or breaking a spell, this powerful herb is a must-have. Rue water is a blessed water infused with the sacred plant, Ruta. It is used to ward off the evil eye, dispel envy, for purification, breaking spells, exorcism, protection from magical attacks, healing, protection from evil spirits and enemies, and protection from night attacks and spiritual illnesses. Ruta is known as the queen of herbs and is native to the Mediterranean area. It corresponds with the planets Saturn and Mars, the element Fire, and with the deities Diana and Hecate. A witch can mix dried rue with blessed water and sprinkle it around the home to remove a curse, negativity, jinx, or to invite positive vibrations.

Rue water is commonly used for purification rituals in Voodoo, Hoodoo, Folk Magic, and Santeria. You can also put some into your bath water for purification, protection, and to bathe off evil spirits.

WHEN TO PERFORM THE SPELL

Full moon

WHAT YOU'LL NEED

- 1 gallon rain water
- 1 cup rue leaves (fresh)
- 1 gallon container
- Cheese cloth
- 1 big rubber band, or thin twine

HOW LONG IT TAKES

Full lunar cycle

CHANT

"Blessed moon,
Lend me your power, strength, and courage to
this water.
A spell of protection here I cast;
The ruta in the water will banish all magical
attacks.
It is done."

STEPS

1. Fill your container with rainwater.
2. Sprinkle the ruta into the water.
3. Cover with cheesecloth.
4. Rubber band or tie down the cheesecloth with
   rope or twine over the container.
5. Put under the full moon, where the moonlight
   is reflected in the water.
6. Just before sunrise, bring it in and cover it with
   a black cloth during daylight hours.
7. Put it back out each night under the moon for a
   complete lunar cycle.

8. At the end of the lunar cycle, strain the blessed and charged rue water into special jars for protection spells and other magical practices.
9. Put some in a spray bottle and spray it on you for protection.
10. Use it to chase away demons.
11. Store in a cool dark place for later use.

Waning Moon Banishing Protection Spell

Moon magic is seen throughout the natural world. Its vibrational energy governs the processes of all changes essential for life. The lunar cycles control the Earth's tides. Two-thirds of the Earth is water, two-thirds of the human body is water, and two-thirds of the human brain is water. So, if the moon can shift the oceans, one can only imagine the influence it has on all living things.

The waning lunar phase is when the illuminated area of the moon begins decreasing. It offers us an opportunity to pause, slow down, let go, cleanse, and release. The waning moon is a time for letting go of regrets and purging anything that no longer has a purpose or what you no longer need. It is a time to sweep out your home, get rid of anything weighing you down, and prepare yourself for upcoming magic.

A waning moon is when the moon goes from being fully illuminated to being dark again. This time of the lunar cycle is used for "baneful" magic or binding magic. Baneful magic gets rid of, destroys, and sends away things that are no longer useful or which are harmful to you. Waning moon magic is suitable for banishing rituals. It is also used for spells that end relationships, legal matters, or even bad habits. Binding in magic is like taking out a restraining order on someone who is out to do you physical, emotional, or spiritual harm.

Cinnamon corresponds with the element Fire, so it comes in handy for all protection spells. I like to use it for my home protection because it has the double advantage of protection and having a wonderful spicy aroma.

You can use this spell to banish something that is harming you from your life, be it negative energy or a person.

WHEN TO PERFORM THE SPELL

Waning moon

WHAT YOU'LL NEED

- Black cord 13 inches long

- Dragon's blood essential oil
- Cinnamon essential oil
- Pen and paper
- Cheese cloth
- 1 big rubber band, or thin twine

HOW LONG IT TAKES

12 hours

STEPS

1. Create a lunar altar.
2. Gather your materials.
3. Create a sacred circle under the waning moon.
4. Focus your intent on what you want to banish.
5. Using short sentences, describe in detail what you want to banish.
6. Tie one end of the black cord, leaving a loop to tighten later.
7. Peer through the loop and read your sentences while tightening the knot.
8. Feel the knot tightening around your words and binding them to the cord.
9. Create five knots in the cord with the same process.

10. The next morning, bury the cord far from your home.

Protection Poppet Spell

Unfortunately, due to stereotypes, Hollywood, and the media in general, many think of poppets as Voodoo dolls. However, dolls have been used in sympathetic magic for centuries. In ancient Egypt, the Pharaoh's enemies used wax images of him to bring about his death.

In both today's and yesterday's magical traditions, sympathetic magic has a crucial role. The concept behind sympathetic magic is that an individual can be magically influenced by spells cast towards something that represents them. In witchcraft, we use connections, associations, and correspondences between magical concepts and inanimate objects or non-magical items. For instance, friendship corresponds to the color pink, green to money, rose quartz crystals to love, and so on.

Some theorize that cave art from prehistoric times might be the earliest recorded example of sympathetic magic. The psychological force behind intent is powerful in the success of sympathetic magic and ritual. The word sympathy means to enter another being's state of mind and feel both affection and pain.

Sympathetic magic uses objects symbolically associated with the person or event over which influence is sought. A perfect example of sympathetic magic is the use of the poppet or doll in magical workings. The poppet has been around for a long time - there is documentation that the ancient Greeks and Egyptians used them, long before pop culture discovered "Voodoo dolls." A doll is used to represent a person, and the magical acts performed on the doll are then reflected onto the person it represents. Using sympathetic magic is a great way to bring about healing, prosperity, love, or any other magic goal you can think of.

A poppet can be elaborate or simple, depending on how much effort and time you want to put into its design. You can use wood, cloth, wax, bread, roots, or clay. Some magical traditions hold that the more time spent in creating your poppet, the stronger the magic becomes. Either way, every part of your poppet symbolizes what you are hoping to achieve. I have a friend who was having a terrible time with an evil spirit, so she made the poppet out of bread and let the birds slowly peck away at it.

If you are using a poppet for banishing, use black fabric and designs such as wands, dragons, swords, or fire. This is a protection spell, so use white or red material with keys, fences, shields, locks, and mistletoe patterns.

Try to make your poppet resemble the person you are trying to influence. Give it two legs, two arms, a head; you can form it like a gingerbread person.

WHEN TO PERFORM THE SPELL

When needed

WHAT YOU'LL NEED

- 2 rectangular pieces of red or white material
- Sharpie
- Small piece of paper
- Needle and thread
- Basil herbs: Protection
- Angelica herbs: Protection
- Cotton balls
- Small bamboo sticks: Hex breaking and protection
- Taglock: Hair, fingernails, and other items from the target's body—if you can get a hold of an old T-shirt or article of clothing or a photograph from your target, use it.
- Draw your own outline or use a poppet pattern

HOW LONG IT TAKES

Depends on complexity

STEPS

1. Draw a human figure on one piece of your fabric.
2. Lay that piece of fabric on top of the other piece and cut an identical piece.
3. Starting with the body, sew both sides together all the way around except for the head; leave that open.
4. Write the target's name on a piece of paper.
5. Stuff your poppet halfway with your herbs and cotton balls.
6. Add taglocks, photographs, and the name.
7. Fill the rest of the way with leftover herbs and cotton.
8. Sew the head closed.
9. Cross two tiny bamboo sticks for eyes.
10. Spend five minutes focusing your intent on your poppet.
11. Charge regularly with sage smoke.

Protection Amulet Spell

Since ancient times, amulets have been major power players in witchcraft, summoning protection with their earthly ornaments and crystals. Thousands of years later, we still use these majestic shields. It is important to bear in mind that just as you and I are made of energy, so is everything in the material world. Your amulet will also have an energy that reflects on other astral realms, so you need to join your energy to your amulet. An amulet is a powerful object that connects you with the higher forces. Its power is based on how much you trust it, since trust produces the vibrational energy needed to power up your amulet. **Note:** You should be the only person to ever touch your amulet, lest someone transfers their energy to it.

WHEN TO PERFORM THE SPELL

Anytime

HOW LONG IT TAKES

1 hour

WHAT YOU'LL NEED

- Handful of sand
- Stone or symbol pendant, ring, bracelet
- Sandalwood or dragon's blood incense
- Black candle
- 1 cup of spring water

STEPS

1. Choose your amulet object.
2. Make a circle on your altar with incense to symbolize Air, sand symbolizing Earth, cup of water symbolizing Water, and a candle symbolizing Fire.
3. Relax and focus, ground and center yourself.
4. Invoke each of the elements, one at a time, place your object on the sand, and chant: "May you absorb the energy of Earth that supports me and protects me."
5. Once you feel the object is charged with the element Earth, move to the next symbol: Air. Hold your object in the fumes of the incense and chant: "May you absorb the energy of air, as air whisps away danger from me."
6. Once you feel the object is charged with Air, move to the element Fire. **CAREFULLY** hold your object over your candle flame. As it is heating up, chant: "May you absorb the energy of fire that burns anything that may harm me."
7. Drop your object into the cup of water, totally submerge it, and chant: "As the water protects, cradles, and hides, may you hide and protect me from anyone or anything that may bring me harm."

8. Now hold your object in your hands, raise it up to the sky, and chant: "I am made of energy, the same energy as the Universe, you and I are united in power and strength."
9. Kiss your object and then breathe on it and chant: "With my breath, I give you life!"
10. Thank the superior elements that govern your amulet as you complete the spell.
11. To clean and charge your amulet, wash it in a clean river or with spring water and salt. Lay it on the ground under the sun to dry.

Spiky Aura Spell

With this spell, you can create, shape, and manipulate your own aura, making it spiky so that you can drive off psychic vampires, narcissists, and anyone else you want to repel. Your aura is an invisible life force that exists as a spiritual phenomenon surrounding you. Much like the energy you learned earlier to visualize after rubbing your hands together, you can manipulate your auric energy in various ways. However, your power to do so is associated with your spiritual strength—not just that of the Universe. Auric energy is molded from your level of spiritual powers through strong emotions and extreme focus.

WHAT YOU'LL NEED

- Sage bundle
- Black coffee
- Cinnamon

STEPS

1. Drink black coffee with cinnamon. It's delicious, incredibly stimulating, and works instantly.
2. Meditate on your intent to spike your aura as you ground and center yourself.
3. Visualize the outer edges of your aura beginning to form sharp spikes. Imagine it becoming electrified. Allow any feelings of anger or rage to tip off the spikes in your aura (it's only temporary).
4. Visualize how your energy is being used to defend you against anything you need defending from.
5. To undo this spell, light the end of a sage bundle and wave it over you and around you.
6. Visualize as you feel into your body and smooth out your aura.
7. Feel it settling down while remembering how to reignite the spikes when needed.

Protection While I Sleep Spell

We all know how it feels when we don't get a good night's sleep, but during your sleep is also when you are most vulnerable to influences from others looking to manifest just about anything they want. You might very well be fending them off throughout your day, but your guard is down when you sleep. You want to avoid any type of magical attack while you are sleeping, which can manifest during the night as restlessness, fear, dread, nightmares, or a complete energy drain upon waking the next morning. Then the attack continues throughout the rest of your day. Maintaining habits for your bedtime rituals can help prevent unwanted attacks. I'm not talking about lengthy rituals, but simply about spiritual maintenance.

WHEN TO PERFORM THIS SPELL

Nightly before bedtime. For extra power, charge all of the ingredients under a full moon.

HOW LONG IT TAKES

7 days

WHAT YOU'LL NEED

- 1 cup of water
- Bowl of water
- 7 eggs
- Salt
- Rosemary

STEPS

1. Keep a small cup of water next to your bed each night to soak up any negative or low energy. **Note: DON'T drink it.** Dump it outside or down the toilet each morning.
2. Lightly sprinkle your mattress and pillow with black salt (just mix a bit of sage ash with rock salt) to ward off evil or bad intentions.
3. Once a week, put a sprig of rosemary in each corner of your bedroom to chase away unwelcome spirits.
4. Each night for 7 days, place an egg in a bowl of water under your bed. **Note: Throw the egg outside each morning!**

Traveling Charm Bag Spell

Travel can be so exciting and adventurous, wandering down mysterious and new roads to discover this beautiful world we live in. Traveling protection magic has always been popular. Some have St. Christopher charms or protective crystals hanging from their rearview mirrors, and others carry amulets or other types of magical talismans.

Think about how much time we spend in our cars, flying on planes, moving about from here to there. Whether we are on our way to the grocery store or out of the state, things don't always go as planned. People lose their wallets, get flat tires, luggage is lost, and people fall overboard! Caution is a must, because we may not have such happy trails if we don't protect ourselves. Just like it's important to have flashlights, water, GPS, and bug spray, we can always use a strong, safe travel spell to protect us spiritually.

WHEN TO PERFORM THIS SPELL

Before travel

HOW LONG IT TAKES

No time

WHAT YOU'LL NEED

- Organza bag, small yellow pouch, or piece of 3-inch square yellow or black fabric
- Yellow ribbon
- Mint
- Moonstone crystal
- Clear quartz crystal
- Picture of a compass
- White camphor essential oil
- Optional: If you have a cat and a whisker has fallen out, use it—obviously don't pull one out for this purpose. Cats use them to navigate and stay safe.

STEPS

1. Place all of your items (except white camphor oil) in your charm bag and tie closed with your yellow ribbon.
2. Dress your bag with white camphor essential oil.
3. Feel the magic growing and building for safe travel on the roads. Hold the bag up to the sky and chant: "Protect this vehicle and those inside. Bless our journey; bless this ride."
4. Put the bag in the glove compartment, and

charge with white camphor oil every three days.

PROTECTING YOUR HOME

Your home's energy is extremely important. You can really sense the energy of a home, especially when it is sad, dark, or haunted. You can also sense the energy in homes that are happy, cozy, safe, and a bit magical. There are many methods of infusing protective qualities into your home. Much of this has to do with what you are drawn to.

Plant Protection

Plants have been used to repel evil in almost every culture in recorded history. Herbs and other plant matter have been used in wreaths, incense, and even scattered around the house for protection. Ancient herbalists, green witches, kitchen witches, and all of us magical folk have valued herbs such as sage, basil, and rosemary for their healing abilities and to cleanse spaces. But they are also strong protectors that drive negativity away from your home. Oregano, thyme, and rue are a few others. Paleolithic gatherers, sedentary farmers, and herding nomads have all been documented using herbs for protection.

Vervain (Verbena officinalis) is also referred to as the Enchanter's herb. Usage of vervain for spiritual and witchcraft practices is traced back to the ancient Romans, Greeks, Egyptians, and Celtic Druids. Vervain protects against negative energy and evil spells. It also purifies your home and other sacred spaces. For magical purposes, grow it right inside your home. Not only does it have a delicious lemony fragrance, but it is also a powerful home protector from unwanted energies. Clip the leaves after sunset or before dawn for ritual purposes. Leave a libation of honey and milk next to your plant after you clip any of its leaves.

Dill is another plant used today and historically by magicians around the world in their charms and spells. In England, it was used to break evil spells when worn directly on bare skin. Hang a stalk of dill in your home and place some dill seeds under your rugs for protection against magical assaults. The aromatic dill plant also protects your home against envious onlookers. It makes sense that dill is governed by the element Fire. Fire is the great protector.

Black iris is great for absorbing negative energy, and it definitely fits in the "witch aesthetic." You can hang some in doorways to protect your home from evil spirits, or hang elder branches outside the entrance to your home to keep unwanted energies from entering;

however, they should hang on the outside of the home, as some witches I know consider them bad luck to have inside.

Water on Your Altar

The element Water has many abilities and forms. It is what makes all life possible and causes it to grow. Water embodies both death and birth, light and dark. It can be unmoving and solid, or it can be fluid. It is the greatest shapeshifter of all. While water is often associated with healing, it is a ferocious element to use in protective magic. There are many methods for using water in protection magic. Some call on the element Water, water itself, or the spirits that reside within the water.

You can keep water on your altar in a chalice, bowl, or cauldron. It creates solutions, purifies, protects, and submerges. Through water, you can bless and charge your altar items—and even slow down time by freezing it. When salt is added to your water, it will erode away all things negative. Most witches keep an altar of some kind, and one good thing to keep there is a glass of water. If the water starts to bubble strangely or disappear faster than normal evaporation, it's a warning sign.

I like to gather all types of water from different sources. I keep little vials with me in case I pass a stream, hit the beach, or find myself in a sun shower. I let my roses sit in water, and then I put rose water in a small shot glass, to which I then add four drops of essential oils. But for protection, I charge water under a full moon overnight. I put out about three gallons, so I have it all month on my altar for the protection of my home.

Protection Powders

Protection powders are an excellent way to provide a protective shield around your home. Some witches sprinkle a line of salt across all of their home's entrances, and others make a blend of various herbs and incense, such as myrrh, frankincense, and rosemary. Salts combined with rosemary are among my favorites because of the sheer strength that rosemary carries. Folklore tells us that hanging rosemary on your doorknobs prevents thieves from entering. Another fav is pulverizing some dried bay leaves and sage into a protective powder and leaving it in a bowl at the entrance to my home. If you are feeling in need of a bit more protection, this blend is a powerful agent for fending off those unwanted energies from entering your home.

Protection Powder Spell

It is important before casting any protection spells that you tend to some magical maintenance chores for your home. The first one is to keep the entranceways clean while also making life more comfortable for your family and guests. Using your broom or besom, sweep your entranceway each morning. You can also add some of the previously mentioned small plants at the entrance to purify its air and make your residence look more inviting. Then make a mixture of lemon juice, vinegar, and water and wipe down all the doorknobs. Then you are ready for this Protection Powder Spell.

Black pepper is used in spells and rituals to banish unwanted spirits and for all other forms of protection. If you want to get rid of a really annoying person or someone who is causing you harm, throw some black pepper into your protection spells. Black pepper corresponds with fire, so it packs a powerful punch of sorcery right at your target!

WHEN TO PERFORM THIS SPELL

Twice per month

HOW LONG IT TAKES

30 minutes

WHAT YOU'LL NEED

- ½ cup sea salt: Universal protector
- 1½ cups black salt: Evil Eye protection, breaks hexes, wards off negative energy
- ¼ cup black pepper: Spiritual protection
- ¼ cup chilli peppers: Breaking curses, banishing, protection
- 2 tablespoons dragon's blood resin: Banishing, protection
- 1 tablespoon garlic powder: Protection from psychic vampires
- A mortar and pestle
- Jar for storage

CHANT

"Protective powder, guard my site.
Send all bad things far away.
Protect our home where my loved ones stay.
These are my words; it is done."

STEPS

1. Using your mortar and pestle, pulverize your materials.
2. While grinding down your materials, visualize

each protective quality they have, and then focus on combining all of their energies so they merge into a powerful protective powder.

3. Repeat the chant three times.
4. Sprinkle protective powder under your front and back doormats and in each windowsill.
5. Store in a cool, dark place. You should have enough for three months if you refresh your sites every other week.

Warding

Warding is a means of protection against all forms of ill-will and negativity that seek to harm your home, you, and your loved ones. It is a type of psychokinetic shield that deflects all harmful activities geared toward or approaching your home. You can cast a ward around the entire perimeter of your home and property.

As with all other protective and preventive measures, cleanse your space and tools to make sure there is no residual nastiness in or around your home. Warding creates an energy shield by visualizing and creating a bubble around your home. Since we are talking about a larger area than just a sacred space or room, you need to be well-rested, as this activity requires intense focus.

Protective Warding Spell

Everything inside of your home and yard needs to be thoroughly cleansed, so there is no energy that you don't want within the boundaries of where you live (your wards). This is a great time to break out an old horseshoe, charged and cleansed to put by your front entrance. There are various methods for warding. You can burn incense, but for this spell, we are going to be conducting energy work.

WHEN TO PERFORM THIS SPELL

As needed

HOW LONG IT TAKES

30 minutes (if you have the house already cleansed)

WHAT YOU'LL NEED

- Two rowan twigs
- Red string

STEPS

1. Ground and center yourself.
2. Tie together your rowan twigs, so they are crossed with your red string.
3. Using visualization, take your crossed twigs and channel your protective energy into them. Envision a tendril coming from you and connecting and entering your rowan twig knot magic.
4. Continue to focus for five straight minutes solely on your intent to protect your home, pushing all of your power into your object.
5. Visualize a dome of energy warding your property. As you create your dome, you will also go into each room of your house and speak to its protection.
6. Feel free to chant or sing while warding. For me, I just submerge myself into focusing on my intent.
7. Once you get to your front door, hang your crossed rowan twigs over the entrance.

Blessed Acorn Spell

Every part of the oak tree is honored in various regions of the world and in some cultures it is even considered sacred. Acorns have been used for protection spells for hundreds of years. Acorns have a rich and deep symbolism in druidry. The word druid literally means "oak knowledge." Oak knowledge is said to be responsible for the Celtic peoples' survival. The acorn, as a seed, symbolizes unlimited potential and growth. Taking two oak twigs and tying them together with a red string, much in the same fashion as rowan twigs, makes a powerful protective amulet. Acorns are usually only a single seed, wrapped in a leathery tough shell that protects the seed, which is why it is such a symbol of protection.

WHEN TO PERFORM THIS SPELL

Anytime, or under a new moon (for added power)

HOW LONG IT TAKES

5 minutes

WHAT YOU'LL NEED

• Acorns: enough for all of your window sills

CHANT

> "On this night, I invoke the protection of the
> acorn
> To wrap my home in a leathery tough shell
> and repel negative spirits and energy
> For I thank the elements Water and Fire
> As it is."

STEPS

1. Chant over your collection of acorns.
2. Meditate on the protection they will provide.
3. Put two acorns in every window sill.

Witch's Spell Bottle

Similar to witch marks (carvings or burned etchings on fireplaces, windows, doors, and any other entrances to homes to ward off evil), which were common in medieval Great Britain, witch's spell bottles were embedded in buildings during the 1500s to the 1800s in the United States and across the British Isles.

For centuries, magical practitioners have been using witch's bottles to protect themselves from malicious spells and sorcery. During the time of the Samhain, homeowners created witch's bottles to ward off evil spirits from entering their homes. The witch bottle is commonly made of glass or pottery and includes sharp items such as bent nails and pins, and sometimes the homeowner's urine to magically connect the family and the property they live in.

The objective of this spell bottle is to not only protect your home, but to send back the negative or evil energy to whomever sent it your way.

WHEN TO PERFORM THIS SPELL

Anytime

HOW LONG IT TAKES

30 minutes

WHAT YOU'LL NEED

- A small glass jar with lid
- Black candle: Protection
- Wine (or urine): Marks your territory
- Red string: Protection
- Sea salt: Purification
- Sharp, rusty items like bent nails, pins, razor blades: Deflect ill fortune and bad luck

STEPS

1. Fill your jar halfway with the rusty, sharp items.
2. Fill the remainder of the jar with wine or urine.
3. Spit in the jar.
4. Tightly cap the jar, and seal it using your black candle wax.
5. Hide the bottle under a doorstep or bury it on the outskirts of your land.
6. It must remain untouched until you replace it once per month.
7. As you approach the bottle with a replacement, extend your hand to see if you can feel a heaviness.
8. Bury bottles far away from your home.

Crystals

Crystals and mineral stones are surprisingly versatile and extremely powerful magical tools. They are used in nearly all magical traditions, including health and wellness spells, healing spells, attracting money spells, and protection spells. Each crystal has a chemical composition unique to it, along with its own vibrational energy signature.

Most witches and mystical workers consider crystals to be "alive" because of the healing energies they provide.

Certain crystals, such as quartz and tourmaline, radiate electrical charges visible to the naked eye when tapped by a hammer. That is tangible proof of their innate power and energy. Since our thoughts and intentions are also energy forms, crystals can be used as conduits to communicate our intentions out into the Universe.

By placing your protection crystals in different places in your home, you can repel and ward off negative or unwanted energies. They work best when placed in the four corners of your yard, house, or apartment. Placing them in this fashion creates a grid of protective energy throughout your home and property.

Charging Your Crystals

In order to successfully use crystals in your magical practices, they must be regularly cleansed and charged. When you charge your crystals, you are essentially adding energy to them, thereby enhancing their vibrancy and power. Charging also raises the intensity of your spells.

- **Moonlight charging:** Leave your crystals on a windowsill or on a flat surface outside directly under the moonlight for 7 hours. Each lunar cycle offers different energies. For instance, full moons are associated with newness, such as when moving into a new home, and new moons are associated with growth, such as new furnishings added to your home.

- **Sunlight charging**: Make sure the crystal you are charging under the sunlight is one that won't fade. For protection, black obsidian and black tourmaline will not fade.
- **Earth charging:** Place your crystals in a jar and bury them in the soil for at least 7 hours or overnight. I charge mine in my herbal planters. You can put your crystals in your garden for Earth charging.
- **Charging your intent**: I use my wand to activate my crystals. First, hold your crystals in the palm of your hand, gently closing your hand into a fist. Close your eyes and focus on your intent to power up your crystals and protect your home. Open your hand and visualize a beam of light stemming from your wand into your crystals.

Cleansing your Crystals

To cleanse your crystals, wave your smoking sage bundle in a counterclockwise direction around your crystals. You can also cleanse them under running water or sprinkle them with salt. Natural light also works very well.

Crystals for Protection Spells

- **Black tourmaline** is a powerful protector. It works against harmful electromagnetic waves that can accompany visitors to your home via electronic devices. Black tourmaline also absorbs any negative and toxic energy and seals your home within a protective shield. One of my favorite ways to use black tourmaline as a protection stone is to manifest energetic boundaries around my home. I create a square boundary around my property and bury one black tourmaline crystal in each corner. If you live in an apartment, you can use the four corners of the interior of your home and place a stone in each corner.

- **Black obsidian** is an absorbent and strong protective crystal. It needs to be frequently cleaned due to how much energy it absorbs, including negative vibrations. It absorbs any dark energies that enter your home. The best placement for these gems for home protection is by all entrances. If you are experiencing any unpleasant energies in your home, double up on your black obsidian and place them there to absorb the unwanted energy.

- **Amethysts** are well-known stones for home

protection. This rich purple gemstone can help repel unwanted or negative energy. Amethyst protects your home against other people's projections and keeps negative energies away.

- **Smoky quartz** has fantastic grounding properties and is also a very protective crystal, so after manifesting your intentions, smoky quartz will block any unwanted energies or influences that may try to darken the energy of your home.

- **Moonstone** is a very effective protection crystal, especially when you charge it with the moon. Moonstone is named the cosmic ruler of the evening sky. Moonstone is an amazing crystal that dispels negative energy and cosmic fog. It has been used as a protective crystal for generations of homeowners, landowners, and travelers.

- **Pyrite,** also known as fool's gold, is my go-to stone to hold when I am visualizing a shield around my house. It will keep emotional vamps from entering your home and cut through negative vibrations, repel psychic attacks, clear electromagnetic field smog, and stop evil dead in its tracks.

- **Clear quartz** is a universal crystal. Not only will it protect your home, but it will also amp up the energies of all your other crystals, items, herbs, and candles. It both deflects negativity and attracts positivity. It is also very receptive, so set clear and direct intentions when you're working with this crystal.

PROTECTING FRIENDS AND FAMILY

Protective spells for family and friends are probably cast more often than any other spells, even than spells for yourself. Wanting to protect your family and friends is a universal need shared among humans as a survival instinct. These spells can be very simple protection rituals or very elaborate.

Onion Braid for Family Protection

Onions have been linked to protective magic for centuries. Making an onion braid is a simple yet effective charm to protect your family and friends while they are in your home. Buy a bag of onions that still have the green tops attached. You also need about 5 feet of twine.

Fold your twine in half, making a loop, and tie a knot near the end. Then lay the twine on a table, and place the greens of the onion upside down, making the third string in the braid. Now you have three strings—two twine and one green onion top string. Next, tightly braid the three strings until your onion is secured in place. Meanwhile, focus your intent or chant for the type of protection you are seeking and for whom you are seeking protection.

"Onions wrapped around a braid,
This charm for protection I have made.
Keep all negativity out of my home;
My family is safe, now I know."

Protection Oil for Your Friends

Brew up a batch of Protect My Friend Oil to anoint your friend(s) with. It will keep them safe from magical and psychic attacks. My favorite blend for my best friend includes ⅛ cup coconut oil, 4 drops patchouli essential oil, 1 drop mugwort, and 4 drops lavender essential oil.

Blend your oils and pour into a small perfume vial or dark glass vial. Focus your intent on protecting the person you plan to anoint, and then tell them to store the bottle in a cool, dark place. Be creative when labeling your oil, such as "Protect My Bestie Oil" or "Protect My Pal Oil."

Protect My Pet Spell

Pets are very much a part of our families; we love them very much. They provide comfort, joy, and companionship and ask very little in return. Pets at home also increase the vibrational energy of the entire house and everything in it, and lighten the mood in their immediate environment.

In ancient times, magical healers cast pet protection spells to keep their farm animals, such as horses and chickens, safe. Today, a spell can be cast to protect our pets, giving joy, positive energy, and long life. This spell creates a small amulet you can attach to their collar.

WHAT YOU'LL NEED

- Black tourmaline or obsidian small crystal (depending on the size of your pet)
- 0.3 mm (28 gauge) jewelry wire
- Scissors or pliers to cut the wire
- Leather piece to loop onto pet's collar

HOW LONG IT TAKES

20 minutes

STEPS

1. Cut two 5-inch lengths of wire.
2. Cross the wires over each other and twist them together in the middle where they are touching.
3. Place the black tourmaline or obsidian crystal onto the wire, with the twisted section on the back of the crystal.
4. Take the wires hanging and twist them around the crystal, making a small basket.
5. Pull all of the wires around until the crystal is secure.
6. Attach it to your pet's collar either with a piece of leather that you looped into the amulet or a small piece of wire you can twist right onto the collar.
7. Focus your intent to protect your pet into your amulet.
8. Cleanse and charge regularly.

CALLING ON AID FOR MAGICAL PROTECTION

Magical Guardians

Magical guardians are spiritual entities that a witch uses to 'bring to life' an inanimate item for protection purposes. This is often the witch's property, vehicle, or home. Witches can become highly connected to these spirits and become able to request a specific spirit inhabit an object. There are many magical guardians in every realm of the Universe. Some say oak trees have magical protection properties, and that is why acorns are protectors. In Japan, there is an 800-year-old camphor tree that people worship for protection and good health. Familiars, sigils, and servitors are three of the most well-known magical guardians known to witches worldwide.

The magical guardian can be just about anything. For instance, if you have a magical guardian for your garden, you can use anything that will not rot away. I have wonderful little gnomes protecting and decorating my garden. A friend of mine drew eyeballs on a rock to protect her home.

Here are the most commonly needed ingredients when constructing a magical guardian:

- Salt water or oil to anoint the object
- Something to represent the elements
- Sage bundle
- Music or meditation if you plan to use your magical guardian to raise energy
- Something to 'nourish' the object (a lemon, piece of bread, etc.)

Sigils

Sigils are a method of magical practice for when you know exactly what you want to manifest. Historically, sigils were a type of picture or design referencing spirits, angels, or daemons. Sigil magic is the practice of creating intention-charged symbols (sigils) to manifest your desires. When creating a sigil, you need to incorporate your creativity, will power, self-reflection, and ritual into your design. It is a way to transform your intention into a symbol to be read by your subconscious as opposed to your conscious mind—much like how you read Tarot.

Steps for Constructing a Sigil

1. Define your intention in one written sentence, using "I am" or "I will be." For instance, "I am protected."
2. Delete all of the repeated letters and vowels: I am protected.
3. Take the remaining letters and start designing an abstract symbol. Try not to concentrate too much on what your creation looks like; let your intuition guide you.
4. Charge your sigil by visualizing a warm beam of energy flowing from your hands and into the paper—or you can clap, dance, or chant.

Familiars

Familiars, also known as imps, are commonly small household pets—but not everyone's is small. My friend has a dog for a familiar who weighs about 70 lbs. Familiars have deep relationships with their witch owners. Legend holds that familiars are loyal guides, guardians, and protectors and they also help out as magical assistants. They are a witch's truest confidant and friend. They see and hear it all; they know us for who we really are.

Familiars are connected both psychically and telepathically when we need them to be. If you are wondering how to find your familiar, well, you find each other. You may be dreaming about a certain pet or feeling understood by one, as though you are connected to it spiritually. If that is happening to you, you have a familiar at your side. You and your familiar are magically bound to one another. It is a very special relationship.

Servitors

Witches can create servitors for protection against magical attacks. Magic lets us focus our energy and intentions, and when externalized, we can create an entity that can help attract the right circumstances and correct energy to allow our magic to manifest according to our desire. One such entity is an egregore, who can bring witches enlightenment, quicker thinking, and opportunities that will bring us closer to achieving our goals. Servitors or egregores have unlimited types of assistance to offer witches, and when your intention is focused, they can manifest any desire.

Witches create servitors as an entity to conduct a specific range of tasks. We intentionally shed portions of our psyche and identify them by means of a symbol, trait, or name. Then we can work with them on a conscious level and learn how they, in turn, affect us. Servitors can work in the form of sigils if the witch can use a complex set of intentions at such a level of sophistication that they appear to operate independently from the witch's consciousness, and if it is an autonomous being, then it is referred to as a servitor. When the servitor becomes large enough that it can be used by a group, it is then referred to as an egregore.

On the other hand, a witch can create servitors from aspects of their personality or mind, such as faults, addictions, shortcomings, bad habits, or revulsions, rather than positive intentions, so they can interact with their own personal demons and banish or bind them to rid them from their psyche.

Some serious rules to consider: be absolutely positive you really want to create a servitor. If they aren't maintained or dismissed properly, you are responsible, and they will try and maintain their existence by latching on to a person. Servitors have a mind of their own, so they can react to situations before you're even aware of them. Always set up restrictions and rules to make sure your servitors remain servitors; without restriction, a servitor can potentially become an egregore, and you will no longer be in control.

Steps for Creating a Servitor

1. Define, state, and write the purpose of your servitor.
2. Create a sigil that holds the definition of your servitor's purpose. "Protect my home," "Cleanse my space," "Keep me healthy," and so on. You can create a series of sigils.
3. Create your servitor's body: Bind them to a poppet, figurine, or your own drawing. You can create a servitor in astral space or in your mind if you don't want to create a physical representation. However, I prefer to be able to handle mine. If you do create your servitor in your mind, be specific about exactly what you want it to look like. What color is it? Does it have hair? What color hair?
4. Bind together your sigils and the servitor's body, and put in its safety rules! You can simply

draw a sigil or carve them into your poppet. Put it where you think its heart is or its battery, as long as you make sure the two are part of each other. Then put in your safety rules. It can be a command such as "Go away," "Begone!" or "Stop!" A servitor must obey the command. You may want to be more creative with your command, since the servitor will obey anyone who shouts the command.

5. Bring your servitor to life! You can have a simple ritual or a full-blown elaborate ceremony. I believe the more elaborate your ceremony, the more powerful your servitor. You can dedicate a candle lighting ceremony, play your favorite spiritual music, adorn it with essential oils and herbs. The ritual performance is the birth of your servitor. Get creative, have a birthday party, and show it around the grounds. There is no right or wrong invitation for your servitor; the more intent you feed it, the better.

6. Servitor maintenance on a regular basis is a must. You cannot forget about it; keep it on your mind at least once a day. If you lose contact with it, it will die. Rewarding it with ritual makes it more and more powerful. It is essential that you know and feel the relationship you have with your servitor. It is

like having a familiar. If you have no safety precautions and you neglect your servitor, you may invite a malevolent spirit to infest your home.

7. If your servitor outlives its usefulness, you need to release it back into the Universe. This is a very humane way to dismantle your servitor, much better than leaving it bound and neglected to perish from a slow loss of energy and death. Create a sacred space, and visualize all of the bindings being lifted and the words falling into pieces and flowing up into harmless light. "You have done well. I set you free." If it seems like it doesn't want to go, perform the ritual again and let it know it is time to move on.

Egregores

Egregores are created in a similar manner to servitors but by a group of witches (like a coven), and they are maintained by the group instead of just one witch. Be it protective, proper, destructive, or evil, there is a broad range of purposes for egregores. They are powerful forces of energy that are always watching and can use their influence to manipulate the minds of anyone, whether the individual is aware or not.

Egregores are independent spiritual beings fed by the focused intent, will power, and mental energy bound by a collective desire of a group of people. Some are evil and have the intellect of wild beasts, while many others are fully conscious and autonomous. It doesn't become an entity without human beings generating its existence. They can only be as evil as the collective nature of the people pulling their strings.

5

REVERSAL MAGIC

W e all find ourselves in tough situations at some time or another. Sometimes, life hands us a dirty deal, and sometimes, those dirty deals have help from someone else's malintent. While ritual and protection magic is the best way to prevent jinxes, hexes, and other forms of magical attacks, reversal magic is the best way to shake them off.

Reversal magic not only breaks a spell cast on you, but it also reverts it back to the person who cast it upon you in the first place. You are basically returning the magic to its original source. It is a safer method than trying to exact revenge. You don't have to worry about a hex backfiring; you simply return the person's negativity back to them.

Not all witches want to participate in active magic that will reverse a bad situation. I have read several books and articles by witches who are actively against any type of hex work. I think taking that position shows naïveté and a lack of witchcraft experience. A witch is very fortunate if they never have to use magic to protect themselves or their loved ones. There are times where protection magic comes down to incapacitating an individual so they can't continue to cause harm.

I think by refusing to work with baneful magic or hexes when they are called for, you are positioning yourself to be unable to protect the vulnerable or oppressed. Sometimes, we can't just sit back and believe that the Universe will deal out justice. As witches, we have a responsibility to act upon injustices.

Defensive or reactive magic is when you are responding to someone else's actions rather than being the one to initiate aggression. It means reacting to malicious actions taken towards you or a loved one and involves reflecting back the harmful actions of another person.

Active magic is when you take justice into your own hands without being attacked first. The hex can be on an institution, a group of people, or on a single person, and is done without waiting for them to "make the first move." Ethical hexing is usually a retaliatory action. An example would be hexing the local drug dealer. Even if the drug dealer didn't directly attack you, you are actively defending your community and family.

Active magic is ethical when it's used on those who are causing harm to people who are oppressed or marginalized. This is known as drawing power or punching up. It is ethical as long as you are not contributing to the oppression of others. But when you use your magic to harm those less privileged than you, it is unethical. Using active hexing should only be conducted when all else fails. If you first tried talking to the person and that didn't solve the problem, using active magic may be the only option. The most important thing to do before using active magic toward another person is to make sure you are targeting the right attacker.

UNCROSSING A CANDLE SPELL

Traditionally, uncrossing rituals were used to remove hexes, spells, bad intentions, curses, and crossed conditions. The goal of this spell is to reverse the malicious intention of another person by sending it back to them. This ritual can also help you to let go of your own negative feelings about that person, and can therefore open you up to transformation.

With uncrossing spells, you will also be cleaning away any negativity held up in your spiritual self. It's like sweeping out the cobwebs and taking back control of your life from whomever is affecting you in a harmful manner.

WHEN TO PERFORM THIS SPELL

When needed

HOW LONG IT TAKES

30 minutes

WHAT YOU'LL NEED

- Black candle
- Pen and parchment paper
- Frankincense incense
- Uncrossing oil: 3 drops vetiver oil, 1 drop cedarwood oil, and 2 drops clove oil

STEPS

1. Write the target's name backwards on the parchment paper.
2. Place the paper on a fireproof shell or dish.
3. Cleanse your area with incense.

4. Make your uncrossing oil blend.

5. Dress your candle from the middle out.

6. Anoint yourself.

7. Light your candle.

8. Visualize all hexes, curses, bad vibes, whatever you are being attacked by as they leave your mind, body, and higher-self.

9. Pour the black wax over the name on the parchment paper.

10. Ball up the parchment paper and bury it away from your home.

MIRROR BOX SPELL

When someone is giving you a hard time, whether it's a boss on a power trip or an ex with bad intentions, then grounding, centering, and cleansing might not be enough for the degree of negativity being thrown at you. Plus, if you are being hexed by another witch, then you *really* need to step up your game.

A simple magical defense spell for this type of circumstance is my Mirror Box Spell. This is a reversal spell that will take any curse from your attacker and flip it right back to them. Again, you must be sure of who you are targeting, and that the feelings are, in fact, coming from within another person.

WHAT YOU'LL NEED

- Black candle
- 2 small mirrors
- Poppet (see Chapter Four: Protection Poppet Spell)
- Shoebox

HOW LONG IT TAKES

One hour

STEPS

1. Cast a sacred circle (see Chapter One).
2. Ground, center, and shield yourself.
3. Consecrate the mirrors with salt.
4. Focus your intention in the mirrors.
5. Light the black candle and set it in front of the mirrors.
6. Set your intention into your poppet.
7. Chant: "This evil you sent will return to you. It's reflected and buried, so no more harm comes from you." Do this five times.
8. Breathe heavily on the mirrors until they are fogged.
9. Place one mirror in the box.

10. Place the poppet on top of the mirror.
11. Place the second mirror facing down on the poppet.
12. Drip black candle wax on the back of the top mirror.
13. Put the top on the box.
14. Bury the box in a small grave away from your home. (The closer to the home of your target, the more powerful).

FREEZER BINDING SPELL

An icebox spell, or freezer spell, is a simple spell to cast. It is the perfect way to stop someone from harassing you, gossiping about you, or giving you a rough time on the job. The use of freezers or ice is fairly common in witchcraft. Many magical traditions, such as conjure and Hoodoo, use freezer spells to get a vengeful rival to hush up or during a court investigation.

In some witchcraft practices, especially spells to stop gossip, practitioners use lemon to symbolize sour words, or beef tongue with a slice cut down the middle. If someone is caught cheating, freezing a vegetable that can be a phallic symbol will do the trick to freeze up their sexual exploitations.

WHEN TO PERFORM THIS SPELL

When needed

HOW LONG IT TAKES

15 minutes

WHAT YOU'LL NEED

- Paper and pen
- Beef tongue
- Twine
- Scissors
- Freezer bag

STEPS

1. Write the person's name on the paper.
2. Using the scissors, cut a slice down the middle of the beef tongue.
3. Slide the piece of paper into the slice in the middle of the beef tongue.
4. Bind the tongue together with the twine, making several ties all over the tongue.
5. Put the tongue in the freezer bag and place it deep in the back of the freezer.

6. Leave it there until the problem has stopped.

BANISHING INCENSE SPELL

If you are trying to banish an unruly spirit, one of the most successful spells to cast is to simply tell it to "get lost!" Chant, being blunt and firm: "You are not wanted here. It's time for you to get lost. Best wishes, but move on."

This simple banishing spell requires you to focus your intent on the spirit(s) you wish to leave you alone. It also requires meditative visualization.

WHEN TO PERFORM THIS SPELL

When needed

HOW LONG IT TAKES

13 hours

WHAT YOU'LL NEED

- Black tourmaline crystal (to charge your incense)
- Basil
- Sandalwood

- Sage
- A botanical gum (to bind your herbs)
- A pinch of salt
- Mortar and pestle
- Distilled water
- Parchment paper

STEPS

1. Crush together basil, sage, and sandalwood with a mortar and pestle until powdery.
2. Add a few drops of distilled water until a dough ball is formed.
3. Mold your dough (½ teaspoon) into cone-shapes.
4. Let dry on parchment paper for 12 hours, turning them over after 6 hours.
5. Place the incense on top of a small pile of salt.
6. Light the incense.
7. Hold the black tourmaline crystal cupped in your hand.
8. Visualize the crystal being a vacuum cleaner sucking up unwanted spirits.
9. Let the incense burn down while it continues to absorb the negative energy.

DRIVE SOMEONE AWAY SPELL

Rooted in African Hoodoo folklore to drive away someone not wanted in your life, community, city, etc., this hot foot powder spell is for bullies, angry exes, relentless solicitors, and abusers who just won't take the hint. Maybe you have tried every passive technique to remove someone from your life, and you finally need to pack a good punch to get the job done.

WHEN TO PERFORM THIS SPELL

As needed

HOW LONG IT TAKES

15-20 minutes

WHAT YOU'LL NEED

- 1 tsp. black salt: Banishing
- 1 tsp. cayenne pepper: Speed, banishing
- 1 tsp. black pepper: Banishing
- 1 tsp. activated charcoal: Absorbs and neutralizes harmful energy
- 1 tsp. habanero powder: Discomfort
- Glass jar

STEPS

1. Using a clean jar, add each ingredient one at a time, visualizing unwanted influences leaving your life.
2. Mix thoroughly while continuing to focus your intent.
3. Chant: "I banish thee. You've crossed the line; for you to go, now is the time!"
4. Store in a tightly-sealed glass jar.
5. Sprinkle in the walking path of your targeted person, around your doorway, or, to stop gossiping co-workers, sprinkle a little by your desk.

RESTORE YOUR LUCK SPELL

Have you ever had a run of bad luck? Does it feel like there is an active curse against you? Ever wonder if you can improve your luck? If you've been cursed or just affected by negative energy, this spell will fix that.

Traditionally, horseshoes, four-leaf clovers, and other naturally lucky talismans have been used to bring good luck. Iron has noteworthy attributes as a protector against harmful sorceries, which is how the lucky horseshoe came about being a favorite charm for witches everywhere. Nailing a horseshoe over the threshold of an entrance to your home is said to keep bad luck out.

WHEN TO PERFORM THIS SPELL:

As needed

HOW LONG IT TAKES

45 minutes

WHAT YOU'LL NEED

- 3 black candles
- Horseshoe
- Hemp cord
- Saltwater spray

STEPS

1. Cleanse the hemp cord and the horseshoe with saltwater.
2. Lay the horseshoe on your altar, points facing away from you.
3. Set your intention to break the curse and restore your luck.
4. Place the black candle in the center of the horseshoe.

5. Light the candle.
6. Visualize the candle flame flowing through the horseshoe and out of the points, carrying away the bad luck streak.
7. Tie the hemp cord around the horseshoe, chanting: "Life is good; luck is back. All negative effects suspended."
8. Repeat the chant for as many times as it takes you to wrap the cord around the horseshoe.
9. Hang the horseshoe with the points facing upward somewhere in your home where you can see it every day.

BEFUDDLEMENT SPELL

A befuddled enemy is much easier to handle than a focused one. We spend a great deal of time bringing positive energy into our lives and the lives of our loved ones, but if you're constantly being attacked, it can be difficult to manage. This spell can help to put confusion into your attacker's mind.

This spell combines candle magic with confusion oil to make sure your attacker is befuddled. Included is a confusion oil recipe that calls for *Galangal,* a twisting herb. Galangal works to create the opposite effect of another ingredient, for example, lavender, so it's use ensures the object experiences no peace or calmness.

WHEN TO PERFORM THIS SPELL

Saturdays

HOW LONG IT TAKES

1 hour (or as long as your candle takes to burn down)

WHAT YOU'LL NEED

- Small black candle
- Salt
- Vetiver root: Breaks hexes
- Lavender oil: Normally brings peace and calmness, but see Galangal properties
- Galangal: A twisting herb
- Burnt knotted shoelace: Metaphorically causes your attacker to trip over themselves

STEPS

1. Tie a pair of shoelaces in a knot.
2. Safely burn the knotted shoelaces and place them on your altar inside the circle of salt.
3. Place your black candle in the center of your altar.

4. Make a circle of salt around your candle.

5. Ground and center yourself.

6. Mix together your confusion oil ingredients.

7. Anoint your candle with confusion oil.

8. Light the candle and speak aloud your intention to befuddle your attacker. Name your attacker out loud, as it is *extremely important* you know exactly who your attacker is.

9. Let the candle burn while you focus your energy on your intention.

10. Scatter the salt into the wind where it will carry a dizzying effect to your attacker.

DOUBLE ACTION REVERSAL CANDLE SPELL

This is a special type of candle that will absorb the attack and send it back to the attacker twofold. If you are sensing that a hex or harmful spell has been cast against you, use this double action candle spell. This candle is double action in two ways: it breaks the hex and simultaneously mirrors it back to the attacker. The red wax melting down over the black represents conquering the evil spell cast on you.

WHEN TO PERFORM THIS SPELL

Waning moon

HOW LONG IT TAKES

As long as it takes for the candles to burn all the way down

WHAT YOU'LL NEED

- Black candle
- Red candle
- Paper and pen
- Reversal oil: 3 drops patchouli, 5 drops lavender, 1 drop mugwort, and 1 drop hyssop

STEPS

1. Prepare your candle. You can buy a reversing candle or make your own by melting the black candle and rolling a red candle in the wax.
2. Carve the name of your attacker backwards into the black part of the candle. This will send the energy back to them because you carved their name the way it would appear in a mirror. If you don't know the name of your attacker

but know you are being attacked, carve your intention forward into the red part of the candle.

3. Prepare your reversal oil.
4. Anoint the black part of the candle in reversal oil while chanting: "I send all negative and evil energy you sent to me back to you, times two!"
5. Anoint the red part of the candle in reversal oil while chanting: "I will it now, release me from any evil spells and send only good things to me."
6. If you don't have a lot of time, use small candles, because you *have* to let the candle burn down for this spell.

DEVIL'S SHOESTRING JAR SPELL

Traditionally, devil's shoestring gets its name because of its long vines. This spell using Devil's shoestring is sure to ward off evil and protect you from bad luck. It works by "tripping up" the devil.

Devil's shoestring is also known as goat's rue, cramp bark, and hobblebush. It works to "hobble" the devil and protect you from harmful energies and magical attacks. This spell will bind up the curse and send it back to the sender.

WHAT YOU'LL NEED

- Jar with lid
- 9 Devil's shoestring roots
- Twine
- Whiskey

HOW LONG IT TAKES

30 minutes to setup, then five minutes every day for nine days

STEPS

1. Tie 9 knots, binding the nine devil's shoestring roots so you end up with a bundle.
2. Fill your jar with whiskey.
3. Place your devil's shoestring bundle in the jar.
4. Leave untouched for 9 days.
5. Run solution through your hair 9 times.
6. Repeat as needed to ward off evil or bring good luck.
7. You can also use it to anoint candles and crystals.

GRAVEYARD DIRT PROTECTION SPELL

The spiritual connection of grave dirt is more about the person buried under it than the fact it comes from a grave. Witches believe grave dirt possesses the characteristics of the individual it was used to bury. Graveyard dirt has been documented in ancient Egyptian times, indicating that they may have used grave dirt and other materials from gravesites, like bones, as part of their magical workings, particularly when it came to necromancy and cursing.

Necromancy is used to deal and communicate with the dead. I have read that necromancy is only performed by powerful sorcerers and wizards, but I know a few witches who have told me they have regular conversations with some of their dearly departed. Necromancers usually have a specific question they want answered or a goal in mind. Their communications are generally intended to uncover secrets and foresee the future. Necromancy has been practiced since the earliest civilizations, and it is still practiced today. Necromancy was performed in ancient Chaldea, Rome, Persia, Egypt, Greece, and Babylonia. It is documented in Homer's *Odyssey*, the Bible, and Ovid's *Metamorphoses*.

It is essential to choose the correct gravesite for spell-crafting. It's best if the person buried in the grave from which you are taking dirt is a family member or friend. This spell calls for a bit of the spirit of the policeman or soldier for protection. You may not have a policeman in your family, but many people have deceased family members who were in the military.

If you don't know the person, make sure you take the dirt in an honorable and respectful manner. First, ask permission. If your intuition tells you the person underneath isn't happy about it, then stop. Make sure to leave an offering of 3 pennies and/or some whiskey or rum. Only take about a handful of dirt, and make sure to express your gratitude when you finish.

WHEN TO PERFORM THIS SPELL

Just before sunrise

HOW LONG IT TAKES

10 minutes to collect graveyard dirt
15 minutes for the spell

WHAT YOU'LL NEED

- 3 pennies
- Rum or whiskey
- 1 handful graveyard dirt
- Salt
- Small pouch or sachet

STEPS

1. Before sunrise, use your bare hands to collect a handful of dirt from a soldier's or policeman's grave. Both of these professions are usually engraved on the markers.
2. Have a discussion with the deceased about why you are taking some of the dirt, and ask permission.
3. Listen carefully to your intuition.
4. When you feel it is okay, place 3 pennies on the grave.
5. Pour a shot of rum or whiskey on the grave. (Don't leave a shot glass there; it might offend someone).
6. Walk the perimeter of your property and sprinkle small amounts of graveyard dirt in each of the corners to protect your home and

property from unwanted spirits and negative energy.

7. Place a pinch of graveyard dirt in some salt on your altar.

8. Place a pinch of graveyard dirt in a pouch or in a sachet and carry it with you.

CONCLUSION

Spiritual energies exist everywhere. They exist in empty spaces, throughout galaxies, within the smallest of molecules, and in the cosmic realm. Negative energy creates static noise that interferes with our spiritual connections.

In our lives, on a daily basis, there are individuals with bad intentions. From the pestering co-worker to the totally obnoxious next-door neighbor, they seem to make life intolerable at times. I'm guessing that most of you have come across people like this. But the good news is that you don't have to turn the other cheek or simply deal with it. Sometimes you can try everything in the book to get someone to leave you alone and back off, but it just doesn't work. This is when magic can help you solve these unpleasant situations. Reversal magic is a way of taking the energies and intentions of another person and returning them to them. Think of it as giving karma a little push with a sealed envelope saying "return to sender"! This book covered this kind of sympathetic magic, as well as bindings, poppets, visualization, raising energy, and showed you how to follow through on your spellwork.

Don't let other people get in the way of the things you want to create. Discussed were numerous ways of cleansing negative energies, grounding and centering yourself, and ways to send back any ill-intent to whomever sent it to you in the first place. I hope my personal stories intrigued you and helped to teach you exactly what to do and how to do it.

Most spells have some influence on the free will of other people, but aren't a bad thing. Magic is defined by changing things. So, unless you're practicing only on yourself, it's impossible to cast a spell without it affecting someone, something, somewhere, somehow. When it comes to magical practice, there is always a chance that someone is going to manifest something by accident. The point is that if you take the time to learn how to work with the spiritual realm, you need to spend the same amount of energy learning protective magic. One individual's "negative intent" is another individual's "getting the job done."

Intention is the most important magical element, but as witches, we like to strengthen and enhance our spells with our tools. Remember to always consecrate and cleanse your space and the tools you are working with. Cleansing your tools and your space is crucial to removing any negative energy hanging about that can mess with you or your magic, so be sure to maintain your cleansing regimen!

Creating a safe home where you can let your guard down and relax is one of the main focal points of protection magic. Some of the oldest magical tools and charms known to witchcraft are specifically for protecting one's land, property, and home. You now know how to keep your home warded. Visualizing a shield around your home makes it difficult for malicious energy to get in. The mirrored aspect of the shield reflects any negative energy back to the sender.

In the end, some of the best advice I can give to you is to not piss off any witches! But if you do, be prepared to protect yourself.